RUTH MOORE

THE TIRED APPLE TREE

POEMS AND BALLADS

ROCKS

The rocks of the earth are its history.
Dinosaur tracks they hold,
They tell what's known of who got here first,
They say how old is old.

Fossil shells on mountain sides
Mark there the depth of seas
That rose and fell with the changing tides
Of numberless centuries.

Creatures came, but not to stay.
Diplodocus lies in his deep.
Time-tried and tossed away
The ammonides sleep.

But not the same are the fossils found
In the Age of Inquisitive Man,
For the tallest mountains wore down to the ground
Three times and are rising again.

Who can write on Time's dust
The secret ebb and flow
Of what roared over the earth's crust
Billions of years ago?

Fierce fires still rage on earth, and within
Rocks shift and fissures crack.
What difference now to who started in
And never did come back?

For the home of Man is already rock,
While his triumphs are shouted and sung,
Whatever volcano or earthquake shock
Tell him how young is young.

The rocks of the earth hold secrets,
Weathered, battered, brown.
Yet a pebble found in a wayside ditch
Might be cut for a king's crown;
And a certain beach-rock, tossed by the tides,
Holds a shimmer all its own.
It takes a polish of silent dark,
As if a black moon shone.

The lapidary who cuts a gem,
Slices his agates thin.
With professional care he handles them,
Finds out what lies within.
For the outside crust of an agate stone
Looks dingy - of little worth.
But inside, when shaped and polished, are some
Of the loveliest colors on earth.

Design is there - mathematical -
A scientist wouldn't be fooled
Over what happened inside a rock
When the gases stiffened and cooled.
But sometimes a difference creeps in,
As the lapidaries know,
When polish shows up a landscape of trees,
With a background of snow.

Or a perfect scene of a big white owl
Sitting poised on the limb of a tree.
What of scientific logic then?
For how could this *happen* to be?

Does some hidden consciousness live in rocks,
Who pokes fun at the human race,
And leaves a portrait for someone to find
Of the devil in hell with flames at his back
And a horrible monkey face?

The lapidary who found this scene
Is thinking, wondering, still.
But nobody has an answer to this,
And I don't think anyone will.

TO HAVE BUT NOT TO HOLD

This is a copy of the first deed,
Written two hundred years ago,
In the graceful and beautiful handwriting of that time.
It is heavy with the language of law
But it leaves no loopholes,
And it speaks for itself now,
As if a single bell-note, struck so long ago,
Had sounded through the centuries
Unchanged.

*

KNOW ALL MEN BY THESE PRESENTS
That we the undersigned, a Committee appointed
By the General Court of the Commonwealth of Massachusetts,
Authorized and empowered
To sell and dispose of the unappropriated lands
    of said Commonwealth,
Lying within the Counties of York, Cumberland
    and Lincoln,
For and in consideration of the sum of Eighteen Pounds
Lawful money to us in hand paid,
By Daniel Gott of Little Placentia Island, so called,
Containing two hundred and twenty-two acres,
And three quarters of an acre,
Also Bar Island, so called,
Containing eighty-three acres, and one quarter
    of an acre -
Both of which islands are situated
Souther end of Bafs Harbor in Mount Desert Island
In the County of Lincoln aforesaid,
Reserving however to each settler who may have
    settled on such Lands,
One hundred acres thereof,
To be paid out so as to include his improvement.

TO HAVE AND TO HOLD
The before granted Premises to him, the said Daniel Gott
His Heirs and Afsigns, to his and their proper use
    and behalf forever -
And we the said Committee in behalf of the Common-
    wealth aforesaid,
Do covenant and agree with the said Daniel Gott,
That the said Commonwealth shall warrant and defend
    the said Premises to him,
His Heirs and Afsigns forever,
Against the lawful claims of all persons whatever -

IN WITNEFS THEREOF we the faid Committee
Have herewith set our Hands and Seals,
This twenty-fifth day of March,
In the Year of our Lord,
One thousand seven hundred and eighty-nine.

SIGHNED, SEALED AND DELIVERED
    in presence of
    Saml Cooper   Saml Phillips, Jr.
    Lillian F. McCleary   John Read
                                   Leonard Jarv
Suffolk:
March 25, 1789 - Personally appeared before me
Saml. Phillips, Jr. and John Read
And acknowledged the foregoing Instrument by them
    subscribed
To be their voluntary act and deeds.

                        Saml. Cooper
                        Justice of the Peace

Suffolk: June 10, 1789, Personally appeared Leonard Jarvis
And acknowledged the foregoing Instrument by him
Subscribed to be his voluntary act and deed.
                              Before Saml Cooper
                              Justice of the Peace

Lincoln fr. Rec August 7, 1789 and entered with the records
for deeds for said County, Feb. 23. trs. Fol. 24G ts.

THE OFFSHORE ISLANDS

The offshore islands belong to themselves.
They stand in their own sea.
They do not inherit; they leave no heirs.
They are no man's legacy.

Blazing volcanoes, cooled and dead,
Marked nowhere a boundary line.
The rise and fall of oceans left
Not one no trespassing sign.

The money was never minted,
The clutch of its greed so strong
It could honor a deed: TO HAVE AND TO HOLD,
And keep these wild lands long.

The first summer people were Indians.
For some five thousand years
They built up shore-line shell heaps before
They lost to the pioneers.

The white man took what he wanted.
He had privilege, laws, and guns.
He made fast his own boundary lines
And his property went to his sons.

From the west they sailed in Chebacco boats,
And the high-sterned pinkys, Essex-made.
In harbors where water was deep enough,
Their schooners carried a coast-wise trade.

The homesteads they made were sturdy,
But those who built near the shores
Had to dig, if they didn't want Indian shells
All over their cellar floors.

Then time slipped by, as inheritance does.
They felt the mainland's pull.
They abandoned their homes to rot away,
And their cemetaries full.

Theirs was the time of history
And written records show
That their hold on the offshore islands began
Less than four hundred years ago.

Now comes the era of real estate,
Of the hundred thousand dollar lots,
Of the condominiums, side by side,
Along the shoreline choicest spots.

What follows the time of developers
No human voice can tell.
But the silent offshore islands know,
And they handle their mysteries well.

They speak with a voice that is all their own,
And this is what they say:
That they talk in terms of a billion years
That their now is not today.
And the ghosts they brought along with them
Have never gone away.

SKIPPER McBRIDE

Down on the clamflats
Of Burnt Point Cove
The hull of an old vessel
Lies rotted away.
There's not much left of her -
Some limp, slimy slats,
That the tide runs over
Every day.

But you can see her ghost
If you know how to guess.
You can trace the outline
Of a long, shallow dip,
Covered half with mussel beds
And mud-cove mess,
Where lie the last leftover signs
Of a centuries-dead ship.

She was no clipper
On the China run.
She was a working coaster
Plugging up and down,
With cargoes of everything
Under the sun,
Hauling back supplies and goods
In a ship-building town.

She might be a mystery
At one with mud and silt,
After two hundred years
Of Time and creeping tide;
But she left behind her history
And the way she was built,
Written down by her builder,
Skipper McBride.

Papers thin and tattered
In an old sea chest
Tell she was the MARY ANNE
Named for Skip's wife.
List of his hand-picked lumber -
He used what woods were best
To build a vessel tough enough
To last a man's life.

Skip didn't buy lumber.
His woodlot was the reason.
First, he cut down and sawed up
His white oak trees,
For white oak, air-dried,
Might take a year to season.
He had time then to ransack swamps
For hackmatack knees.

White pine masts, two sticks
Sized and dressed,
Smooth as the skin
On Mary Anne's back.
Yellow birch for underwater work
Always the best,
That never would rot,
That no jolt could crack.

Skip wrote about a tree, just right
For what he needed,
But under it he found
Hidden in the puckerbrush
An old campsite,
With a lot of Indian arrowheads
Scattered on the ground.

"Signs of an Injun tribe
Drove off and gone.

Let the undergrowth have it
Keep it where it be."
He walked out around it
And then moved on.
"Be damned if I'll use that one.
It ain't a lucky tree."

He carried his own lucky piece,
A gray-dark fossil stone.
The sailor he bought it from
Didn't want to let it go.
Said it meant long sailing
For any man to own.
The little critter in it lived
A million years ago.

Skip wrote about the sailor,
"Likely he lied,
So's he could put his price up
Make me think 'twas right.
But that talk about a million years
Kind of stirred me up inside.
I asked him what the critter was,
He said, 'An ammonite.'

"I asked him where he come from,
He said he was a Greek.
Damn furriner or nothin,
I paid his price in gold,
For that little curled up critter
Done everything but speak,
Said, good luck and long life, and
Old, old, old."

Somewhere offshore
In the tricky Gulf of Maine,
Buried deep or water-worn,
However drowned men go,

Are the bones of Skip McBride
Lost in the hurricane,
Called, in the records then,
The century's worst blow.

It smashed up the MARY ANNE,
Left her a wreck,
Drove her toward the coastline
Before the mighty blast.
Skip and two sailors washed off her deck,
Trying to cut the rigging
From a floating mast.

Two weeks later,
The mate and three men,
Sailed her home on jury-rig,
A hope and a prayer.
She was too racked out
To go to sea again,
They grounded her on Burnt Point flats
And left her there.

They brought ashore her logbook,
Along with Skip's chest,
It turned up in someone's attic
Some fifty years ago.
Skip's last entry was,
"The weather's turning west.
Come on, you goddamned ammonite,
It's time for you to show."

The mate wrote up the logbook,
A few short notes
That told about the hurricane
And how Skip died;
About sailing home
With their hearts in their throats,

And the vessel half-sinking
On each change of wind and tide.

Skip McBride's lucky piece
That told him what would be,
Doesn't speak of luck now in tomorrows
Unknown.
Says only, lost, forgotten, gone in the sea -
The little curled up critter
In its nest of dark stone.

THE ANGEL

At our house
We fed the winter birds -
The chickadees who stayed
Through any weather,
The foolish ones
Without the sense to fly
When all the flocks took off
And went together,
The crippled ones
Who couldn't go fast or high.

We kept our sheltered
South yard shoveled free,
With a narrow footpath
Leading through the snow;
Set rocks to brace
The wild birds' Christmas tree,
So it stood tall
Whatever winds might blow;
An open invitation
To the sky
For hungry northern
Travelers, flying by.

The tree had been our own
Till Christmas Day,
Building bright-colored
Promise, guesses, hope.
Of course we knew
That relatives away
Would send the usual
Handkerchiefs or soap,
All wrapped up fancy.
Anyone could see
So they'd look expensive

Underneath our tree.
We had them spotted
And we didn't care
Too much for socks
Or itchy underwear.

But surely, one year,
There'd be something new,
Enchanted, wonderful
That stood apart,
With all the mystery
Of dreams come true -
The gift ungiven
Stored in the secret heart.

Whose gift to us
It was, we couldn't say.
What it might be
We didn't even know.
It would be last
Tucked in and hidden away.
It would be beautiful,
The tree said so.

We'd open bundles
Full of things and things,
Until we knew this year
Would be the same.
Nothing was left
But cranberry-popcorn strings,
And Grandmother's sad old Angel,
Dingy, lame.
And she *was* old.
She'd come a pilgrimage.
She'd been on Grandmother's
Grandma's Christmas tree.
And earlier trees than theirs.
She showed her age.

Nobody knew how far back
That might be.

In some forgotten time
She'd dropped a wing,
That, years ago,
Had been stuck on with glue.
It was always coming off
Had to be glued again.
She was too fragile
To be sewed with string.
The one who handled her
Was Uncle Ben.
He was clever with his fingers,
Could fix up anything.

Seemed there was nothing
That he couldn't do.
He could play the banjo,
Make up his own tunes, too.
In the tough times
When things looked dark and grim,
It was as if the sun came out
And shone on him.

He knitted a hammock
Out of bait-bag twine
Laced the Angel in it,
Gentle with her wings.
She didn't look too holy or divine,
But she always hung there
At the top of all the Christmas tree things.

We were used to her.
When Christmas time began,
We were too busy
To glance up that high.
Or if we did

She was only old Ragged Ass Ann,
The name the boys made up
To call her by.

On Christmas mornings
After the shining tree
Had broken all its promises
Was when
Without its load of hoped-for mystery
It turned back into
A plain old tree again.

We wouldn't miss it.
It had had its turn.
Pa said thank God
He'd dodged it long enough.
Each time he filled the woodbox
His big stern
Got trimmed with Christmas balls
And tinselly stuff.

And Ma was glad
To see the holders down
That clipped the lighted candles
To the tree.
Now that the boughs
Were dry and turning brown
She was scared of fire
As anyone might be.

Grandmother stripped
The cranberry-popcorn strings.
Berries and corn
We scattered on the ground,
With barn-floor chaff
For birds with crippled wings,
So seeds were there for them
And easily found.

We took off all
The fancy trim and tied
Food-bags for birds
Among the falling sprills.
By the time we got the tree
Braced up outside,
Chickadees lined
The kitchen window-sills.
Through frosty windowpanes
With heads together,
Then we ourselves lined up
To see the show.
Strange birds might come
Depending on the weather.
We always hoped to see
The crippled crow,
That had a missing foot,
And one white feather.
He'd stopped there first
A number of years ago.

That feather made him wonderful to us
But he had no friends among the other crows,
They chased him off
And squawked and made a fuss.
All he could do
Was dodge the pecks and blows.
So we made a special place
Not near his brothers,
And fed him by the doorstep
When he came.
After awhile, he didn't go near the others,
We didn't scare him
And he got quite tame.

II

One Christmas morning
Uncle Ben was late.
He'd got up early
Crossed the Bay to town.
"I bet he's gone ashore
To celebrate,"
Pa said. "Come on,
It ain't no use to wait.
Let's shake a leg
And get that darn tree down."

That was the year
When George would turn fourteen,
The age when any boy
Could own a gun.
He prayed that Christmas Day
Would bring him one.
He didn't pray
To Santa Claus because
George was too old
To swallow Santa Claus.
He didn't pray in secret.
We all knew
That what he wanted
Was a .22.

His prayer went out
To Pa and Uncle Ben.
He talked it in his sleep
And time and again
He got up nights
And hunted everywhere
If Bill kept tabs on him
George didn't care.
If they had bought his gun
He had to know

But he couldn't find
A single clue to show.

Of all the snoops we knew
Bill was the worst.
No matter what your secrets were
You found
That Bill's sly, picked nose
Had found them first
And he couldn't wait
To peddle them around.
He was our brother, ten years old,
But still,
Sometimes we wished
Someone would strangle Bill.

One night, up-attic,
Last place in the house
George had to look,
He found a crazy mouse,
That ran across his bare foot
Squealed and hid.
He dropped his flashlight,
Hollered like a kid,
Forgot his .22
And all his prayers
Stumbled and rolled
The length of the attic stairs.

He wasn't hurt.
Neither was brother Bill,
Who was snooping from the hatchway
Keeping still,
Nosing around, as usual
On the scent.
George plowed right over him
And down they went.

When Ma looked in
To see who'd made the howl,
She found us all asleep,
Or so it seemed.
But Bill spoke up.
"You must've heard a owl,
Or George's nightmare,
Something that he dreamed.
It scared him so
He fell right out of bed.
I guess he made the bumps and thumps,"
Bill said.

"Uh huh," Ma said.
"So long as no one's hurt.
And your thumps and bumps
Don't keep us all awake.
I won't ask *you*
Where you rolled
In all that dirt.
Now, go on back to sleep,
for heaven sake!"

So George was done.
He'd rummaged everywhere.
If they'd bought his gun
They'd squirreled it away.
He hadn't missed a place.
It wasn't there.
And it wasn't on the tree
On Christmas Day.

George sat there glum,
Not joining "Oh" and "Ah."
He ripped out socks and ties
And all his "trash."
He didn't see
The big, wide grin on Pa,

All he could think of
Was his dream gone smash.

When Uncle Ben at last
Got back from town,
We didn't see his boat
Come in to dock.
We'd got the tree set up
And anchored down.
There were lots of birds
And it was ten o'clock.
We had the bird book out
Trying to see
If it told who the strangers
On the ground might be.

Bill saw him first.
He couldn't wait to run
And holler up the stairs
Where George had gone.
"Hey, Georgie-Porgie,
Turn your nightmare on!
Unk Ben's got back,
And HE AIN'T GOT YOUR GUN!"

Pa reached for Bill,
"You cut that out!" he said.
"This started out for fun,
A Christmas joke.
We kidded George a little
About his gun.
Now, thanks to you,
It's all gone up in smoke.
I ought to take you out
And spoil the rod,
While Ben shows George
The way things meant to be.
He's coming now, and -

Oh, Almighty God!
Do you kids see outside there
What I see?"

We hadn't. We'd been watching
Pa and Bill,
Wishing that Pa
Meant every word he said.
It would be great
If the smarty-pants little shill,
Got walloped in
A session in the shed.
But Pa, being Pa,
Had been known
To whack the wall,
And say, "Okay, you squat
Down here and bawl."
He was too easy-going
To spoil the fun.
In all our lives,
He'd never licked anyone.

All right with us,
And Bill didn't need to care.
He pushed past Pa.
He couldn't wait to see
That Uncle Ben had come
And was standing there,
Looking up
At the bird-trimmed tree.
And with him Aunt Liz Brown,
Po-faced and grim.
She'd caught him up ashore
And had crossed the bay with him.
What he was looking at
With Aunt Liz Brown,
Was, we'd forgot to take the Angel down.

Grandmother lived with us,
Great-Aunt Liz was her sister.
Grown-ups and kids, we
All called her "The Blister."
She did her best
With all her might
To haunt our holidays.
Nothing on earth
Was ever right
But her own works and ways.
She nagged and hassled everyone
It always was the same.
We all of us had to move over
When "The Blister" came.
And once she got herself
Settled in,
For weeks she wouldn't stir.
The only thing that
We could do
Was stay away from her.

She came in like
A thunder squall at night.
Bill yelled, "Hey, look!
No gun, Pa. Who was right?"
"This time you'll listen,
You little nut," Pa said.
And he scooped up Bill
By his pants-belt,
And ducked out into the shed.

"The Blister" didn't stop
To shed her things.
She opened up and said,
"For heaven sake!
Your cranberry popcorn strings!
Left-over bread!
And all them junks

Of scrumbled up good cake!
Stuff you could've et
Or fed your pig.
I never see such
Heathern-wicked waste
For the sake of some half-witted
Backyard rig.
And I never knowed our family
So disgraced!

"I see you've had your Christmas,
Couldn't wait.
Well, it wasn't me
It was Ben here,
Who was late.
And what he done,
He got likkered up in town,
His breath stinks bad enough
To knock you down.
If I'd got here
Soon as I planned to be,
I could have stopped
That sinful blasphemy,
Hanging our Angel
On that old dead tree!"

Grandmother, never one
To mince her words,
Said, "That was done
On Christmas morning, Liz.
We thought our Angel
Might remind the birds,
About whose Happy Birthday
This one is."

When Grandmother spoke
A quiet word,
We never answered back;

But seemed Sis Blister
Hadn't heard.
Just her corset steels took up
And answered, "Crack!"

"Please listen, Liz,"
Grandmother said.
"That tree is dying,
It'll soon be dead.
And one sad thing
On earth, it seems to me,
Is the last struggle
Of a suffering Tree."

Now Uncle Ben
Wasn't really lit.
He never drank more
Than a little bit.
A swig or two
Made him singing-happy
Or singing sad, as the case might be.
He took over from Grandmother
Started a song,
Making it up as he went along -
A sad song for the Christmas tree.

"It can't live long.
Its roots are cut.
Where it was is only
A bleeding butt.
And this is its only chance to know
The feel of cool
When the cold winds blow.

"Remember warm
In the summer heat,
The wild birds' dance
On their tickling feet.

The fading memory of standing high,
A green candle
Against the sky."

His voice flowed smooth and simple
On the air.
And when it stopped
A kind of peace was there.
The kind you find
On woodpaths, in the breaks,
Or slack-tide just before
The ebb tide makes.
When no wind stirs the water
On the beach.
We didn't have it long
With Uncle Ben
Before The Blister
Started in again,
The same old chawmouth
And the same old screech.

She snorted, "Rob your pig,
And starve your cow!
And as for Ben,
His foolish trash will keep.
What I want to know, right here and now
Is where in all this meally
I can sleep."

Ma tried. "Oh, dear!
We haven't got a bed,
The kids have grown a lot
Since you were here.
Even the parlor sofa's full,"
She said.

"I s'pose you think
I'm going back to town
Just for the lack
Of some place to lie down.
Won't hurt one of your kids
To double up.
You got any coffee?
I could use a cup.

"My head is aching hard enough
To crack it.
And I'll thank you kids
To stop your cussid racket!"
She grabbed her suitcase
Started up the stairs.
One look at Ma
Told you who needed prayers.

Grandmother winked at Uncle Ben.
"Hi, Santa Claus, I'm glad.
We couldn't think
What held you up in town.
You'd better hunt up George,
He'd teen-age mad.
Which pantsleg have you got
His gun stuffed down?"

"This one," he said.
"Mine's in the other boot.
It's God's green wonder
I *didn't* go on a toot.
I wasn't sure how long
You folks would wait,
And of course we wanted
The rifle on the tree.
It ain't my fault
I had to be so late,
But old Sis Blister

Climbed all over me.
I tried to wait her out. I tried to dodge.
But nothing worked.
Oh, dammit! Poor old George!"

George wasn't poor.
He was half-insane with joy
He was a Man with a Gun now -
Not a boy.
He grabbed the gun
And rushed outside to shoot,
While Pa unloaded
Uncle Ben's other boot,
And sat right down
To sample and enjoy.

We at the windows
Saw the birds go by,
A cloud of panicked wings
Against the sky.
The last one left
A crippled chickadee
Creeping to hide
Under the Christmas tree.

George came back in,
All blooming and a-glow.
"I gotta learn
To aim this gun," he said.
"Know what I done?
I fired at a crow
And blowed old Ragged Ass Ann
To hell instead.
You bring back any more
Cartridges, Uncle Ben?
Shoot! I'll have to go ashore
To try her out again."

The bangs outside the house
Had started war.
Inside, we all began
A screaming towse.
George yelled, "Hell's bells!
What's a new rifle for?
You little kids shut up
Them squawks and yells.
I didn't have no other place to go.
The woods all round is up to my neck in snow."

Aunt Liz came down
Plunk-plunk, from stair to stair.
She was all winged-out
Rigged up in coat and bonnet.
She sailed herself
Straight to the nearest chair,
And stately as a queen
She sat down on it.

She screeched at Ma.
"I cannot stand this noise.
I never, ever saw
Such awful-acting boys.
That one a-squalling
Out there in the shed
Is making yowls enough
To raise the dead.
I'll have you know
I wish I hadn't come.
Ben, you git up there
And fetch my suitcase down.
If you can walk that far,
You drunken bum.
This's the last straw.
I'm going back to town."

Outside, you could have heard
A feather drop.
Inside, we could have done it
With a pin.
Then the woodshed door
Banged open with a slam
And Bill bounced in
As happy as a clam.
Pa hadn't licked him.
What did we expect?
He'd just been out there
Howling for effect.

Bill started in by showing, then,
What *he* had to show.
He and Uncle Ben were the only ones
Who could Jump-Jim-Crow,
So he began his jumping bit
Across the kitchen floor
Yelling the rhyme that went with it
As loud as he could roar.
"First upon your heeltap,
Then upon your toe.
Turn about and twist about
And Jump-Jim-Crow."

Creak! went the corsets,
As The Blister stood straight up.
"I asked you for some coffee.
Didn't even get the cup.
You ought to've had some ready.
I needed something hot.
I'm dizzy and unsteady
These is *heart-pains*
I have got."

Grandmother looked at Lizzie.
We could tell she'd had all

She could take.
When she turned that quiet
Gaze on you,
You couldn't make any mistake.

"You've had heart-pains
Before, you know,
That didn't turn out to be,
Times when things didn't go
Just so.
So don't come that on me.
Right now we're pretty busy,
And we *don't* have an extra bed.
If you're really sick and dizzy,
And don't feel able to walk,
The boys'll put you onto a sled
And haul you down to the dock."

Uncle Ben with her suitcase
On the stairs
Said, "Yes! and you'll have
All our prayers.
We'll be glad to rush you
Back to town,
And see you safely
Settled down.
As you know, the nearest doctor
Is over across the Bay."
Then Bill, our Bill,
Our precious Bill,
Had another word to say.
"They couldn't bring over a casket.
They'd lug you off in a basket,
And 'twould spoil your Christmas Day."

The Blister was caught
In her own trap.
She tied up her bonnet strings

With a snap.
Past the birds' lost Christmas
We saw her go.
Past the roughed-up blobs
Of blackened snow,
Where the shredded bits
Of the Angel lay.
She walked in fury and didn't see
Angel or bird or Christmas tree.

Grandmother said,
"That was really rough.
I'm sorry but one of us
Had to get tough.
Lizzie's puddin-stick's
Always astir.
The devil himself
Couldn't live with her.

"That heart-pains trick
She's used before.
Thought it would stick
Just one time more.
Time after time,
As I recall.
She wasn't planning
To leave here at all.
I haven't a doubt
That the poor soul's lonely.
We could put up with that,
As we have done. Only
This time we can't
Have her live with us.
All that rant
And all that fuss,
When we have our own trouble
To straighten out,
And get us back

On our wings again.
Which we couldn't do
With her raging about."

She leaned and glanced
Out a windowpane.
"Lizzie'll recover.
She's only cross.
Well, kids think it over -
There's no great loss
Without some small gain."

III

George learned very fast
What a gun was for.
You didn't waste bullets
Or start a war.
Or let off a blast
In your own back yard.
He learned how to aim,
And George worked hard.

Through long, cold winters
When hard times came,
George kept us going
He brought home game.
In the hunting season
Every year
He never failed
To get his deer.
We had rabbits, wild duck
And venison,
Coot-stew running out of our ears,
Hope kept alive in starvation years,
From the hard-working muzzle
Of George's gun.

As the years went by,
He got well-known.
In time he outgrew his .22,
Bought a .30 .30
All on his own.
With that, he could drop
A chicken hawk,
Flying not too high
In the sky.
And the hunting men
Began to talk.
Then all at once
He was really great,
He won shooting-matches
All over the State.
At shindigs and fairs
Crowds gathered to see
His gun drive a nail
Stuck into a tree.
Wherever it was
He had to go.
And he brought home cups
And trophies to show.

Like the lost Angel
We never found,
Like the crow with one white feather,
Like the birds who fled
The rifle crack,
Gone in the sky together,
George went away
And never came back.
He was truly our Man with a Gun.
Standing tall in a battlefield.
He died in World War One.

WOODCHUCK

The woodchuck slept in the ground.
His burrow was dark and deep.
Furry and small and round
He rolled for his winter sleep.

Beech leaf crackled and curled.
Grass withdrew under snow.
Ice covered the world
But the woodchuck did not know.

What of the foolish crows,
The rabbits bitten with chill?
He put his paw to his nose
And dreamed of a night on a hill,

With the moon over a tree
And cornstalks tall and fair,
And a far off sound of sea,
Like a sound out of the air.

REMEMBRANCE OF A DESERTED COASTAL VILLAGE

The land goes back and it was hard to clear.
Hay-fields, sweat-watered once, are green and lush,
But not with hay - with spruces, everywhere,
With alders and the immortal puckerbrush.

Here once were houses, barns, a pasture gate,
And there the Indians' shell mound, choked with sand.
Five thousand years were not too long to wait
For those who come at last to claim this land.

A little sliver on the end of Time
Unhinged the doors, dropped walls and dried the wells.
The stubborn seeds drove up through lath and lime,
The tough wild roses hid the weathered shells.

Secretly, now, beneath the secret leaves
The essence of forsaken things is blown;
Secret the hanging spider as she weaves,
The golden flies above the cellar stone.

Oh, come away from here for seagulls standing
Stiff-necked and still on their old hip of ledge
Have given us little welcome for our landing,
And he forgets if he be ghost or guest,
Who stays too long upon this echoing edge
Of rock, among the scanty marsh-grass thinning,
To watch the web of water, spinning, spinning,
Past these old ruins, lonely and possessed.

FORT ALICE - A LEGEND
1812

This old stone wall along the harbor side
Is grayed with moss, but fallen only where
The growing trees have shouldered it aside.
These rocks were chosen well and piled with care.

Flat stone on flat, and all the niches filled.
Someone named Alice made it, in the years
After her menfolk went away, were killed
Sea-fighting with the English privateers.

For years, they say, she walked the beach alone,
Bent double by her apron-loads of stone;
And folk at night looked shoreward from the town
To see her lantern bobbing up and down
Till square and strong, the tons of rock she lugged
Were made a wall, and every gap was plugged.

And then, behind it, standing, on her lips
Curses, she aimed to sea an ancient gun,
Watching by night and day for British ships
That never came, because the war was done.

RETURN

They shoveled it in
Unresisting, dumb and blind,
To lie in a black hole of darkness
Time out of mind.

Then into the earth that is now its heart
The root of the tree
Gentle, pushing, inquiring,
"Where are you now?
Where can you be?
Come with me?"

Slowly around the foot of the deep-based boulder,
Thrusting aside here a stone and there a stick
Up past last year's withered grasses,
Matted, thick . . .

And then, suddenly,
Exploding, blazing, flaming
Into the springtime sun.

Oh, kindly earth that held so long in trust
These lost, wild juices
Now at last set free,
The leaves that burn like green fire in the maple
Cry out
Victory

TWO COUSINS - TWO CENTURIES REMOVED

I

Within her beats the blood of nameless men
Who sought far countries, trod the decks of ships,
Unblest adventurers, with reckless lips,
And eyes that looked on shores beyond her ken.
They went their ways, did not come back again.
She sews strange patchwork, while the gray day slips,
In savage patterns, thinking as she snips
Of distant seas, calling her now, as then.

The old fierce fires that in her flamed so fair,
Glow with unquiet embers still. She makes
Designs of dreams, cloth memories of rare
Wild venturings she never undertakes.
She stays at home, and age is with her there
Like twilight falling on the Bitter Lakes.

II

Strong traffickers, her fathers sought with bales
Strange, crested islands, green among the bays
Of reef-set seas, and tide-torn waterways,
Along old coasts mapped out in ancient tales.
Sunburnt, sea-wearied, wracked by tropic gales,
They searched the inland river's hidden maze,
Or down the sea's vast hillside, through the haze,
Fierce-eyed, saw pass the pirates' rakish sails.

Precise and parasolled, in mellow brown
With thin lace cuffs to lend a proper tone,
She minces gravely on the road to town,
Seeing across the bay, a ship, wind-blown,
Her brother's squat black schooner, coasting down
To Boston, with a load of quarry stone.

MARCH

March comes in crazy.
She can't think what to do.
She draggle-tails old Winter
On behind.
She knows the days of ice
And frost and snow
Are few,
But nonetheless,
She can't make up
Her mind.

"Shall I stay Winter?
Or shall I bring Spring?"
She pokes herself
And tries one on
For size.
"Right now I'll show you
What I'm *going* to bring:
Zero. Black frost.
Blizzards. Howling skies.
I'll sneak behind old Winter's doors
And let them slam.
I'm coming in like a lion
So I am.

"You coons go back to bed
And go to sleep.
You earwigs better find
A hole that's warm.
Squirrels, mice and rabbits
Dig in deep,
For I'm stirring up
Tornadium and storm.

"Some of you menfolks took
Storm windows off too soon.
Some of you uncovered
The outdoors water pump.
(Ha . . . ha)
Now you'll see sundogs
And a ring around the moon,
And all the dirty weather signs
I am going to dump.

"This that I'm saying
Is an All-Points-Bulletin.
I'm giving you a warning
And you'd better
Move fast.
Anything you've left outdoors
You'd better rush and
Pull it in,
For there's no way of telling
How long this blast
Will last."

Then March sat down
For a few moments' rest.
She almost went to sleep,
Then woke up with
A jerk.
A monstrous black cloud bank
Was low down in the west,
And it looked as though
This trial-try
Was building up
To work.

She heard the wind let out
A shrill, squawking squall,
As if someone had trod on
A tomcat's tail,

And all of the menfolk
Were hustling by the wall,
Covering up with plastic sheets
Seedling box and pail.

The setting sun looked
Like an egg
That had busted
In the pan.
A handsome rainbow sundog
Was just slipping
Out of sight.
"I've got them all a-going,
Shaking a leg,
They'll finish up what I began
Now I can sleep
All night."

March found a tall tree
And in it she hid,
She went to sleep hearing
A thunderous
Grating roar
Across the offshore ledges -
Her answer from the sea.
Then she was too sleepy
To listen any more,
Only to think,
"That roaring sound is me.
I came in like a lion.
So I did."

The owl returned to its thicket
And the moving life of the wood
Went back to tunnels under roots
And the nests beneath
The wall,
Where the flat foundation stone

A silent guardian stood,
And took care of them safely,
Mice, earwigs and all.

March woke up next morning
And slid down the tree.
She did a little
Yawning,
But felt no surprise.
The lovely spring daylight
Was what it ought to be
Not a ripple on the ocean,
Not a cloud in the skies.

The wind smelled of growing,
A sweet passing breeze.
Spring was here
And showing
With no lies or doubt,
And she could hear
The rustle,
Around among the trees,
The hustle and the bustle
As all her friends
Came out.

She wiped the sleep-seeds
Out of her eyes,
Honest as water-weeds
She gave herself
A poke.
"You scatter-brains don't
Recognize
A little early
Spring surprise?
What were you so scared of?
Can't you take a joke?

"You know how I come leaping in
With my cupfuls of weather,
Good or bad
When I begin,
All wovelled up
Together,
So when I told you yesterday
I'd come in like a lamb
You foolish folks
All ran away
Bug down and hid.
   I am not irresponsible,
I certainly said, 'lamb.'
So I did.
And here I am.

Crazy old March,
With your weather in a cup.
Don't lie to us -
As if you didn't know.
That green spot
In the garden,
Is a crocus coming up,
Where blew your last thin scarf
Of powdered snow.

JOAN OF ARC

Cool maple leaves in early morning dew,
The rabbit's thumping foot and bobbing tail,
The crow's untidy nesting place, I knew,
Nothing of marching feet and coats of mail.

I tell you simply, judges in your wrath,
I am not wise, I have no golden tongue.
I mind I stood beside a forest path,
And watched the pheasant leading forth her young.

I call to mind that when Saint Michael spoke,
There was no sound of trumpets in the sky.
The dewdrops shone as clearly in the oak,
The pheasant was not frightened; nor was I.

God's saints do not come down to us, my good
And noble lords, like kings of earth arrayed.
It was a simple meeting in a wood.
To tell me what to do, and I obeyed.

CATHERINE OF ARAGON

Tufted peasant and crested don
Clutter the streets with their gossiping,
Catherine, Princess of Aragon
Sets forth to marry the English king.

Twenty ships with embroidered sails
Carrying treasure from southern seas,
Carrying laces and costly bales
And casks of coin from the Pyrenees.

Twenty sails in the sparkling sun,
To the sound of cannon setting forth,
Bearing the dowry of Aragon
And peace to the king in the murky north.

Catherine, royal, and very young
Did she look back at the churning foam
As the great blue shoulder of ocean squng,
Over the fading hills of home?

HELEN THE PRINCESS

Helen the Princess when she was young
Knew wild blossoms and palace flowers,
Watched the silver swans as they swung
Around the foot of the castle towers.

She dreamed no dream of a far-off town
Or topless turrets tumbling down.
Helen the Princess strolled among trees,
And saw bright sun on the wings of bees.

East wind, west wind, spring and fall,
Brought strange ships to the shores of Greece.
Minstrels sang in the castle hall
Salty songs of the golden fleece.

In the market-places where goods were sold
Travelers rattled their rings of gold,
And the castles looked down past sheets of foam
At the galleys of Troy returning home.

Wild in the sky the trumpets pealed
Calling the clans from near and far -
Agamemnon, his mighty shield,
Menelaus, his horse of war,

And the great ships heeled to the thundering wind
With vengeance fast to the banners pinned,
For Helen who smelled of palace flowers,
And watched the swans from the castle towers.

JULY

Under the summer sky in peaceful midnight,
In the face of the full moon,
Before the turn of the tide,
Seals, dogfish, pollock, mackerel, all sea-hunters of prey,
Drove a school of brit into the shallows of the cove.

The little fish, frantic, in terror,
Fled, crazed, into the only way they could go.
They plunged headlong to shore, died in windrows,
          gasping, on the beach.

Then,
Out of ledge-crevices, holes in sand,
Out of the green-black sea-bottom woven with
          tide-sucked matted weed,
Countless crabs came, scrambling sideways to the feast.
Claws clutching, mouths gobbling,
They made no sound.
Except for a slight commotion of spray as they crossed
          the edge of water to the sand,
They were silent;
But their wet backs returned bright sparkles to the moon,
And the beach looked as though invaded
By a colony of undersea black stones,
Which had somehow come alive and were moving there.

The tide turned, gray-green, ice-cold.
In the light of morning,
The beach peas rustled in the small breeze that
          comes with dawn.
Trees on the bank quiet, drift still, slight ripple on
          the water.
Land weeds in the clearing flattened with dew.

The clean and empty sand lies under a peaceful sky.

INSCRIPTION FOR AN H-BOMB

Here am I
Who have smashed all your microscopes.
I have brought you perpetual winter;
But give me credit -
I have also cured your hatreds forever.

MARCH FIRST - CABIN FEVER

Since there would be no peace
But underground,
Harry
And Jane
And John
Nabby
And Fred -
Some fancy in her lost
Befuddled head
Had whispered "Oleander"
As a sound
Lovely as June to call
Her new-born by.

She lay and said it over
To herself.
"It's bowls of cream
Along the pantry shelf.
It's pretty places
I won't ever see.
It's like a fern.
It's like a flowery tree.
It is a flowery tree
I've heard somewhere."

Trees full of blossoms
Misted in her mind,
Courageous blossoms,
Falling on the air,
That turned to snow
Before they touched the ground,
For Henry coming in
Was not aware
That the door's opening
Let in a sound

Of winter-booming breakers
And the snow.

He blundered often
But was not unkind.
His eyes were agony
To see her so -
Dying in wintertime
And he to blame
And with no words at all
For comforting.

"Henry, you'll mind?
About the baby's name?
I've called her 'Oleander,'
Come the spring.
It's 'O-le-ander,' Henry,
Don't forget."

He nodded, looking bleakly
At his hands.
"I fed the chickens.
The's one broody hen.
One cussid broody hen
That wants to set."

Never the sight or sound
Of him again,
His children's crying
Or his daily bread
Or any trifling need of his
Could win
Her back again from what
She saw ahead -
A peaceful place
To put her body in.

The frozen land, the blue
Intolerable sea,
Looked back at her through him
Across the bed,
Until the branches
Of a flowery tree
Blossomed again and shut them out,
All three,
And everything that he
Had ever been.

Shaken with sorrow
That could not be kept,
In solitude, at last,
Or any place,
He leaned the gray December
Of his face
Over the cradle where
The baby slept;
Until the other children unaware
Came creeping through the door
And found them there.

AMELIA GOTT TELLS ABOUT HER GREAT-GRANDFATHER AMOS

My cousin Julia is a thing-reader.
She can take hold of an object belonging to someone she doesn't
        even know,
And tell you where it's been, or what the person's like -
Or was like, if he isn't living now.
Because, she says, a spirit's in the thing
That tells its story. She can feel it through the skin of
        her hands,
A humming, like.
Suffering, she says, or any great strong feeling, soaks into
        things like dampness,
Which explains haunted houses and walkers in the graveyard
        and poltergeists.
So *she* says.

I don't know.
I've heard a lot of stories, most of them humbugs.
A good ghost story can curdle your blood, but all the same
        it's kind of enjoyable.
Me, I've thrown spilt salt over my left shoulder many a time
        to keep off witches,
Not that I ever knew any, it's something you do, just in case;
But I never saw any poor unfortunate tarryhooting around the
        cemetery in a white nightdress,
Which I don't believe a sensible spirit would do.
If any of my menfolks should ever come back
After such a journey and in whatever shape,
It wouldn't be the cemetery they'd head for.
It would be for the dinner table and the nearest cup of coffee,
Or where's the rum bottle?
I told Julia. She's considerable younger than I am,
So I can say about what I want to, to her.

"Julia," I says, "Why don't you lay hands on Great-great
Grandfather's
          sextant there on the mantelpiece,
If that's whose you think it is,
And tell us where he come from in the first place.
We've always wanted to know.
We don't go back past him.
And if your spiritual powers can tell us where he's buried,
Maybe we can go look at the place,
Or find out something about him that's so."

Now, that was real mean of me - not to shade things.
Because you could put in a pepper-shaker what's known about
          Great-great Grandfather Amos.
There's only one item that seems as if it might be true,
Passed down to all of us who bear his name.
He was a butterfingers. He Gott-ed things up.
Even now, if we make a mistake or have a plan go wrong,
Somebody's sure to say, "Gott-ed that one up, didn't they?"
I won't say we do it every time.
I only say some of us are likely to.

Julia huffered right up. She's a great one for ancestors.
"We do so go back past him," she says.
"And if you'll stop your clack long enough for me to get into
          the swing of it,
I'll tell you in a minute where he come from and where he
          went to."
"So do," I says. "I'm listening."

First she shut her eyes.
Then she hove a long sigh, stopped with a noise like a burp
          as if she had a bellyache.
I almost said, "Julia, have you got a bellyache?"
But seeing of the way her hands were feeling of the sextant,
I held it in.
I'll wait, I thought, and see what she come up with.

"I see him," she says. "I'm beginning to see him.
He's a tremendous, tall, broad, strong boy,
And he's got yellow hair."

Well, that was no great shakes for a spirit to come up with.
Most of us now - our family's known for it -
Are tall, big-footed people with gold-colored hair in a kind of
          bush,
Except for some, including me, whose hair is straight as a
          string and black as a coal.
Julia got the yellow.
And I thought, She ain't in a trance, right now, any more
          than I am.
She knows perfectly well what she's doing.
She's rubbing it in on me about that Passamaquoddy Indian
Who got tangled up with us somewhere back along.
I opened my mouth to say so, but she got in first.

"I see a great stone castle beside the sea," she says.
"And he's telling me who it belongs to -
The Royal Dukes of Dorset, that's who.
What he's saying is we're all descended, straight down
From the Royal Dukes of Dorset, England."

Trust you, Miss Ancestors, I thought, to come up with royalty.
Troddling around in the past, the way you do, it was a fore-
          gone conclusion.
"My!" I says. "Was all them Dukes the first ones to Gott
          things up?
Or does that go on back past them to some King?"

"It's possible," she says.
"And very likely," I says. "If the King, them times, was George
          the Third.
He Gott-ed things almighty up, if you ask me."

She never said what she thought about that
But went right on, as if I hadn't spoken.

"Our Great-great Grandfather settled here in 1785.
He built a house - that's his cellar hole in the back field we've
        always called the old potato hole.
He went in sailing vessels.
But this spirit don't know what vessels they were or where
        they went."

"I should think," I says, "That if this sextant was his,
Along with the sea chest and the three books of navigation
        that we always knew for a fact belonged to Great-
        Grandfather Walter,
It certainly ought to know."

That brought her out of whatever fuzz she was in.
She opened her eyes and give me a mean look.
"They *was* Walter's. Passed down. They was his father's first.
When, I ask you, did Walter ever go to London?
He was a Grand Banks fisherman, remember.
And if you'll read what it says on the pure ivory of this sextant
You'll see it says, G. YOUNG AND CO., LONDON.
Now, you listen to me, Amelia.
Things around a spirit has got to be sympathetic,
And right now, they ain't.
This spirit has stopped speaking."

"Why, they are, too, sympathetic," I says.
(I was dying to know what other glories she'd come up with.)
"Tell him excuse me, if what I said was wrong."

"All right," she says. "But from here on out you watch your
        tongue.
I ain't trifling and neither is this spirit."
And she hove another long sigh and started over.

"Great-great Grandfather had eleven children, all of them girls.
One after another, as fast as he could put one into his wife."

"What about Walter?" I said.

"Has the spirit lost count, or was Walter a woods' colt?"

"It's coming to Walter. She was due of her twelfth, and
          Great-great Grandfather left home."

I couldn't help myself. "And time he did," I says.
"If there's strong feelings coming through that sextant, I'd say
          they'd ought to be his wife's, poor thing.
Telling how she hoped to God he'd left for good.
Did he?"

"No, he did not. He went down to the shore and started choring
          around in his fish-house.
The fish-house sounded as if he was fighting a bull in there.
Long about noon, one of the neighbors came by,
Stood at a distance and hollered to him.
'What's the matter with you, Amos? Your wife's had a boy,
Don't you know it?'
And started to run as the side of the fish-house began to
          bulge out.
Amos didn't bother to come out the door.
He walked straight from where he stood at the time and
          appeared at his wife's bedside
With the wall of the building draped around his neck
And the head of him out a window."

I could have said I'd heard that barnacly old yarn before and
          about somebody else,
But I could see more was coming.
So all I said was, "His wife, what was left of her, must've
          thought he'd Gott-ed things up for fair, that time.
Was that where the butterfingers stories started?"

"Oh, no. That started with the WILLIAM CAREY."

Now, I'm seventy-four to Julia's forty-eight,
But I thought, right then, she's slipping before her time.
Or maybe she thinks that what with hardening of the arteries

which I've got some of,
I wouldn't remember about the WILLIAM CAREY.
Or that it was Great-Grandfather Walter who Gott-ed that one
up.
The WILLIAM CAREY was a British barque, of London,
Bound from New Orleans to St. John, N.B., via St. Thomas.
And what happened to her took place in 1863,
Written up as an item of history in our local paper,
December 4, 1896.
I've got the clipping in my scrapbook.
In the Gulf of Maine, she ran into one of the worst tornadiums
the people of the time remembered,
And she anchored three miles outside our Harbor here, in the
tide's way, distress signals flying.
Great-grandfather Walter called for volunteers,
He got together a crew for a dory and they rowed out and
boarded the WILLIAM CAREY.
Had quite a time doing it, what with the tide and the gale
blowing on.
Walter took charge, told her captain to slip chains and he'd take
her into one of the safest harbors on the coast.
They came in flying hellity-hoot past the outside ledges,
Before the wind, like a bird, on the wing.
It turned out that in his scramble up the coast
The Captain had had to slip a number of chains.
The only anchor he had left was a small one;
But he'd thought coming into "one of the safest harbors on
the coast,"
He wouldn't need more than that. He hadn't told Walter so,
And Walter hadn't thought to ask him,
Or to tell him that in a southerly the wind bulled up the "safe"
harbor like through a funnel.
That light anchor, when they hove it over, didn't even make
the WILLIAM CAREY hiccup.
She piled up high and dry on the Harbor beach.
All hands were saved, along with her cargo, which was mostly
made up of runaway negroes. She was a total loss.

I let Julia tell it that far, and then I said,
"Oh, *I* know quite a lot about the WILLIAM CAREY.
She was a hundred years old, built of teak, a wood that never
          decays.
She carried the first missionary to India and was named
          after him.
The mahogany captain's-dresser with all the nice little
          drawers came from her.
You're sitting in front of it, right now, Julia.
And the stair-rail and banisters in this house are made of teak
          from the WILLIAM CAREY.
I guess you've forgot that my house now was Walter's house
          once.
You laid hands on them banisters the very day you went upstairs
          to fossick around in my scrapbook."

"I did not so do that," Julia says, like ice.
"I never knew you had a scrapbook."
She got up, put the sextant back on the mantelpiece and left
          the house.
I haven't seen her since.

About a year after that, my nephew Walter came home on leave
          from the Navy.
World War II, he'd been all over on an aircraft carrier.
Told about his leaves in London and other English places.
Travelled all of them in them double-decker buses,
Looking England over, seeing what things was like there.

I was reminding myself to ask him more about what them
          big buses looked like,
When I come to, like an owl in a tree, because I heard him
          say this:
"Rode out one day to a monstrous big stone castle they let you
          go in to see," he said.
"All plastered with gold and silver stuff and treasures of one
          kind and another,
And pictures painted in color of a lot of the kings and dukes

they got over there,
And you know what, Aunt Amelia?
Them pictures of what they called the Royal Dukes of Dorset
Looked just like me. Crazy, wasn't it?
There was one young fellow, about twenty-five he looked to be,
Who was the spitt'n image of Cousin Julia, only of course,
        a man.
Yellow hair and all, and them pink cheeks she used to have
        when she was somewhat younger.
I felt pretty foolish, when the guy who was with me went back
        and spread that all over the ship,
And everyone started to call me the Royal Duke of Dorset."

I thought a little. "You must've wrote Cousin Julia about that,"
        I says.
He grinned as he got up to go. "Shoot, Aunt Amelia, you know I
        didn't," he said.
"You must have heard folks carrying on something bountiful,
Because the whole war I never found the time to write a letter
        home.
I don't write good enough so's anyone can read it anyway.
Well, back to the salt mine. See ya next time, if there
        is one."

He took his yellow hair and his pink cheeks out through
        the kitchen door,
And after a while, I went back into the parlor and lifted
        down that sextant.
There it was, old, somewhat beat up, and the strip of ivory that
        was printed with G. YOUNG & CO. was coming
        unglued.
"You never told Julia where you was buried or what become of
        you," I said to it.
"And maybe, considering, it's a good thing you didn't have time
        to.
I wouldn't want to have you any closer than you are."

REFERENCE LIST

At the place on the coast where I had a garden,
Of a summer afternoon, the sounds were these:
A redstart,
A catbird, teasing the cat, meow, meow.
Some chickadees.
A heavy marine engine, off somewhere.
Traffic - not much, this time of day.

Wind, a light breeze in the spruces,
Hushing in the Siberian iris.
These like this garden. There's a damp spot where
          they do well.

A flick of wingfeathers, a thump, which is a robin landing.
She can't wait. She's put out.
She wants me to go away so she can get at the strawberries,
Knows very well that she's the only one I say, "Boo!" to.

A song sparrow,
A sleepy hum of flies.
Another engine, the big one on the dredge in the harbor,
Sometimes it makes a sound of lament.
Sometimes it bawls like a bull.

Voices from traffic, where the road from the dock
          joins the highway,
"Step on it, will ya? God, you'll never git home!" A tenor.
The answer, a slow baritone: "Well, then, for chrisesake, go by."

An oven bird - "Teacher, teacher, teacher."
A seagull, far off, sleepy.
A winged bug, close by my ear, buzzes, stops, then
          flies away.
A warbling bird-song, ending in a sound like water
          dropping on water.

I don't know who he is.

A crow.
Two crows.
From somewhere in the woods, an answer.
Then a whole flock of crows, yelling like witches.
They have got something. No, something has got
            one of them.
There goes a big hawk who has taken a crow,
Whose brothers aren't having that without a fight.
Murder scene, quickly played.
They are all gone now, out of sight in the trees
            behind the garden. I'll never know who won.
Leaving
An outboard, starting up, gasping, stopping.
He flooded her.
Sam Peabody, the white-throated sparrow,
He doesn't sing often this time in the summer,
But here he is, with his lovely flute.

A crash of wood on wood, almost like a rifle shot,
Somebody uptown's unloading lumber, dropped a two-
            by-four, like.
Something in the grass making a small sound like a
            creaky mechanical gate.
"Widdley, widdley, widdley." Sure, I know you.

A deep humming toot, like a liner's shortened whistle.
The dredge, saying it's quitting time; in a moment
            they'll drop the last scoop into the scow alongside.
And there it goes, rattle, rumble, splash.
The harbor'll soon be bigger, deep enough for summer yachts,
But all I can think of is, what a waste of living
            clams and mussels.

A child, walking with his mother on the path that passes
            the garden, says,
"What's for supper, Ma?" and she answers, "Chicken."

The child whines. "I won't eat it. I thought you were
                going to have something nice. Like hot dawgs."
Whoever said that little children's voices are always sweet?

It is late afternoon. Gasoline engine time.
The lobster boats, draggers, handliners are coming in.
Healthy commotion at the end of a working day.
Diesels, outboards, inboards, Bitey Plug's big one
                has no muffler. He likes the noise, he says.
You can always tell when he comes by the Head.
Now, a day's catch sold, boats back on the moorings,
Car doors bang down in the fish wharf parking lot.
Tired men are heading home for supper.
They had a cold lunch. They're hungry. Supper's always
                early. Ready for them.

Sun's dropping low in the west, setting clear.
Be a good day tomorrow.
I wait at the edge of dusk for the hermit thrush,
He sometimes sings quite close to the back of the garden.
There he is, now.

THE MEN WITH GUNS

As they walk forth in the sunshine of
Their sacred immortality,
Their blood flows smooth as honey or love,
Or autumn rain on a gallows tree.

As they walk forth, as they walk forth,
The wild birds whistling down from the north,
The salmon at the river's mouth,
The fleeing deer, east, west, and south,
The fear-struck squirrels as they climb,
The mothers of growing daughters and sons,
Will learn the savage sound of their guns,
Whose hands are on the helm of Time.

LITTLE RIVER

Little River lighted-whistle
Cry no more.
Sleepy sound from the breakers calling me
Back to shore.
     Whistle it soft to the silver river,
     Whistle it loud to the drumming sea.
     Whistle it low to the moon and morning.
     Not to me. Never to me.

For I'm swinging high in another country
Swinging low,
Playing it cool and the dolphins follow me
Where I go.
     Whistle it loud to the flood tide making.
     Whistle it soft to the wheeling sun,
     Whistle it wild to my girl's heart breaking,
     She'll remember, she was the one.

Spring comes warm over Little River,
Storms come black.
I was headed home when the Indian Giver
Took me back.
     Whistle it high to the graybeard breakers,
     Where the secret over the great shoal ran.
     Whistle the world that was in my pocket,
     When I had pockets,
     When I was a man.

BLUE ICE AND GREEN WATER

Oh, Blue Hill Bay, old Blue Hill Bay
She's a handsome sight to see at any time,
She can sleep in that old sun
Where the winds of summer run,
Shine in winter like a bran-new silver dime.

      But don't trust her, boys,
      She's wide and she's deep,
      Don't mean what she says at all;
      Down along her cold ledges
      The sea crabs creep
      And the kelp it does grow tall,
                    boys,
      That kelp it sure grows tall.

At four in the morning the lobster boats go,
The seiners come in from the south,
She can shoot back the sun like an I-beam of gold,
And butter won't melt in her mouth.

      But check on your sparkplugs
      Make sure you've got gas
      And gear that won't crumple or crack,
      For every three years
      She takes a man
      And she don't ever give one back,
      Not one does she ever give back.

You can call out the Coast Guard
To set off some flares,
And hunt till your eyes drop out blind.
Blue ice and green water is all you can see,
Blue ice and green water
Is all you can find.

   Blue ice and green water
   To the end of the land.

SEPTEMBER

Work gravely in your garden,
Charles, your child
Beside you, tawny-headed
In the sun,
Waiting for windless dusk
To burn the piled
Old autumn leaves, before
Your work is done.

You watched the garden bloom
In the summer heat,
Weeded and hoed, gathered
In morning light.
Now the rubbish is cleared away
And smoky and sweet
The flower of your fire
Will blossom against the night.

The seed will be here,
The stem and the leaf - all here
The spirit to smoke
For the winds of the sky to keep.
While a man goes home
From his work in the fall
Of the year,
To his house and his bed
And the peace of
His winter sleep.

"FOR IT MAY BE THAT GOLD IS NOT ALL"
(Hakluyt's Voyages)

O curious man, whose faith is in his dreams,
Whom God will not content, nor a small house,
But who must range the planet, finding there
Unshelter, where his heart cannot abide.

For centuries, his bones lay listless,
Runnelled by Time and frost.
No crow picks at them now. There is little to find.
Today the wind furrows his land of dreams -
Wheat in Dakota, snow on the High Sierras,
In Alta California
A boy who would have been his centuries-great-grandson
Plants a tree.

South from the Straits to Terra del Fuego
Through all that lonely coast,
There was no Northwest Passage. None.
Chesapeake might have been, or Hudson's Bay,
But the great gulfs narrowed down, became swamps or rivers.
So far the keels could go, and then no farther.

Ship after ship was lost; many men dead
Among the 18,000 islands to the north,
Seeking the Passage which must be surely there,
But seemingly one not navigable for ships.
The *Half Moon* did not sail it; she did not sail Gatun Lake.
She is a patched canvas memory,
Vanished down the horizon of a more terrible sea.

PART ONE

I

In a counting house in Amsterdam, the rosy merchants,
Rotund with generations of good beer,
Cloaks ermine-lined, thrown back, caps furred to stop the
          draft
Satan devises for seeking out bald heads,
Sat listening unmoved, except by a ponderous anger,
To the young man whose hands were quiet,
In bandages curiously white on his rough, brown fingers;
Though there was not much else about him that was quiet.

"Spring was already sweet in the English counties,"
He said; and shrugged impatiently,
As if he could not be too quickly done with spring.
"But north of Orkney, off the coast of Friseland,
We found foul weather, cold rain, sleet and snow.
I wish you might have been there, gentlemen,
To see how fast, with that gale abaft, we sailed.
It would have done you good."
He smiled a little wickedly into their silence,
          thick enough to have dropped a stone in.
"Good, I mean,
For you to have seen how expeditiously we ran our
          westing down.
You would have said so swift a voyage would prosper.
No?
Well. She's a good ship, your ship.
You'd not believe how soon she raised the ice-blink."
Gerbrandus stirred.
"In language that is less commendably poetic,
Captain,
Tell us what the ice-blink is.
We are all landsmen here."
"Not all, I think," said Pieter.

He was a little man, almost a dwarf,
Lost in his carved oak chair.
His head was big and shaggy, like a dwarf's,
With tangled, hairy brows, and under them
Gleamed an astonishing pair of sea-green eyes.
Gerbrandus grunted. "Who's the sailor? You?"
          and Pieter said, "Oh, pouf, Gerbrandus!" rocking and
          rolling on his small pointed stern.
"Gerbrandus has a pain," he said. "His wallet hurts.
That means he aches all over, the whole man.
And what an ache that is. So he calls names.
Tell him about the ice-blink, captain, and go on!"
The captain did not turn his head.
Doubtless he had already seen Gerbrandus' vast magnificence,
The satin waistcoat rounded like a promontory,
And having seen it once, remembered it.
He said,
"A field of ice reflects a light against the sky.
It can be seen for miles, when a ship approaches it
          from sea.
It tells you where the ice is, or, at least, that the ice
          is there."
Pieter said, "Has it a color?"
Something in his voice
Made the quick eyes swivel toward him.
"It is like a rainbow's ghost, or a horizon that is all
          one sundog."

"You found no gold there, no mineral of value?"

"The coast is bitter cold. We could not land
For many days, because of a marvelous great commotion of the
          tides and sea
Which flung the ice floes upon one another.
We anchored within the sound of that great growling.
The fog there is quick.
It comes in like a coverlet flung down."

"You did not land because of fog?"
Said Behrens.
His fingers stirred the flat links of gold about his neck,
Following the smooth metal downward toward his belly.
There was comfort in that cold caress,
But Behrens' stomach was queasy,
Thinking of his lost investment, the disaster of this voyage.
"We had high hopes -" He sighed. "Our hopes too high
To learn they have been defeated by a . . . a mist."

"Gentlemen, I have tried to make this clear to you.
There is great hope in this undiscovered land.
Who knows what lies behind those capes and headlands?
I tell you, they stand a thousand feet of stone and ice,
Beaten upon by the mightiest sea that I have known.
You have not believed me,
And you will not believe,
Unless, by a miracle, I could show you what is graven upon
                              my remembrance,
The wondrously carved great pieces of green ice
Flung in the air a hundred feet and crushed to crystals,
Showering back to the sea and flashing in the sun.
I tell you, the Queen's Foreland is the rampart of a continent.
But what lies there, what metals -"
He paused, his eyes on Behrens' vest,
"What *minerals of value*, I know not.
I know that the people there are wild and cruel . . .
They have strange tortures.
I have no proof that they have gold."

"You were ashore, then?"

"I was, my friend.
I had, as you know, an English crew.
I left there five dead men.
At least, I hope they are all dead,
For we found only three to bury.
That I have come back and brought you home your ship,

A little scraped about the keel, but whole,
Is a healthy fact not altered by my personal terror of
                    the . . . mist.”

“The ship does not replace
The gulden we invested.”

“None the less, you are lucky to have her.
I regret that I have not made your fortunes, gentlemen;
And your reluctance to equip a second expedition
Which might go far to mend them;
But more than all I regret the necessity of giving up
The bravest vessel I have ever sailed.
You will not reconsider your decision?”

“You have brought nothing back.”

“No, and again, no.
The fruits of my shore expedition consisted of some eggs,
                    fowls, and a young seal,
All these, alas, were eaten by hungry men.
But I have in my pocket three small stones
Brought up in the tallow from soundings.
You see they are worthless,
But they are round and they shine like gulden.
Unfortunately, there are not enough for all of you.
Fight for *them* gentlemen!”

He flung them down,
Turned from the table blindly and went out;
The heavy door echoed his departure.

At the gate leading into the snowy street
He felt his sleeve pulled, lowered his eyes,
Colder than ice and black with disappointment,
To Pieter, the little, ancient map-collector,
Who had put on his galoshes before following him.

"You must learn tact, my fiery young friend,
Before you try to handle business men.
It is my opinion that they are very sensitive now,
And do not love you much."
He cocked his shrewd face of a small, fat gnome
A little to one side, stared up unwinking
Into the remote bleak eyes above him.

"Amsterdam is chilly tonight, and bad for my gout."

"As the cold weather off the Queen's Foreland was bad for
          mine.
In fact, my foot itches, my fat friend."

"Come home with me," said Pieter. "On the day I go to God,
(And may it be far off), I shall be glad to put my soul to sleep
With the thought that once I gave a brave man
The marvelous good dinner he deserves."

"My thanks.
I think your meat would choke me."

"Oh, tush! My meat is the best in Amsterdam,
As good as your manners are bad.
Besides, for twenty months you have eaten my meat
And are unchoked,
(Though I confess that the salt beef I spent perilous great sums
          upon,
To fill the casks for your damned unfruitful voyage
Was not the quality which you will eat tonight.)"

As his pocketbook remembered,
Old Pieter forgot his shrewdness, began to hop with rage,
"Blast you, come home with me!
At least I can hear you talk.
Do you think, you feverish fool, that you can come
Back from the most wondrous adventure yet known to man
And walk away from me with the tale untold?

Why, I will hear that saga about the icebergs,
And how your men died,
Or I will do the kicking and send the seat of those
                    ill-favored pants of yours
Into the nearest gutter.
Are you coming?"

"God knows, sir, it would not take much of a kick.
I will come with you, and thank you."

They walked together through the wintry streets,
Seeing upon the snow the comfortable lamps of Amsterdam.
Great loaves of bread unloading from a van
Gave out to the cold air a smell of brown and sweetness,
Lights streamed from windows, and the bells of sleighs
Tinkled stout burghers home.
Outside old Pieter's house, a lantern burned
Casting a lilac shadow on the snow,
Inside his slippers warmed before his fire.

II

"I tell you, I will not sit beside the fires
These fat old men have built to warm their world.
There is something to be found outside the circle of that light,
And I will go back and find it if I sail there in a pinnace.
It is a savage land, full of cold and desolation,
Men die there horribly,
As I have told you.
I sped the soul of my ship's boy, William Tamfield;
He was sixteen, a fair lad, full of courage.
I pulled the arrow out of him and he died.

"It is a marvelous arrow, tipped with stone,
And in its shaft a wonderful gray feather.
I have it in my cabin, it still has blood upon it.
I do not know the people who made that arrow,

We never saw them. Sometimes in the dark
We saw their fires across the snow,
Sometimes we heard a cry, human, but like a wolf howl.
Two of the men I lost we found loathsomely tortured.

"I do not wish to revenge myself on these people.
I wish to know them.
I do not care whether or not they have treasure . . .
If they have, in any case, it belongs to them.

"In the days of our sojourn upon that coast
We could not go far inland,
We could only make a few tracks in trackless snow."

He rose, tramping the floor, his heavy boots
Making marks upon the polished tiles.

"I tell you, I must go back.
I must see what the land is like behind those foothills.
I cannot rest until I have tasted the salt again of that ocean.
If I find gold, tell your fat friends they are
                    welcome to it.
There is something there besides gold. I do not know what it is.
I must know.

"I must know whether that great desolate sea which I have
                    discovered
Opens to the Indies on its farther side;
And there I am at one with you, my friend.
Tell them they must equip another expedition.
I must have that ship.
I know how she sails.
I know what she will do in a field of ice.
Oh, damn their tallowy souls for not letting me have that ship!
Promise them I will get their thrice-cursed silks and spices for
                    them.
There is a continent behind that ocean,
God knows what it holds,

But I will know.”

Old Pieter listened to the curses roll
Across the shocked air of his unaccustomed room,
Until the tankards tinkled on the wall.
His eyes were on his beer,
As if it were an ocean, unexplored,
And unknown what might rise from its pale foam.

“Sit down,” he said at last, “my peppery friend;
The English navy has singularly gifted you.
Our Lord-God-Jesus would be pleased
Could he but make his own name so impressive.

“I am old, I know, and my soul is fat,
As you so tactfully have said.
God help us both, you are a dreamer and you have no sense
                    of money,
And a jackass would have a better notion of how to handle
business men.
Had I but had your chance this afternoon
To tell the story which you have to tell,
I would have come away with thirty ships,
And gulden enough to sail them off over the edge of
                    the world.”

He paused thoughtfully. “You did not tell them you have
                    discovered a great inland sea.
And that . . . is just as well. Brackish? . . . yes.
H’m . . . The mermaid you saw afloat on the icy water . . .
Could she be caught and brought back here to Holland,
A million gulden would be paid to see her.
Your men who vanished . . . they may still be alive -”

“They are dead.”

“But if they are not, who knows what they may have found
Of wonders or of treasure?”

Sadly he wagged his head, set down his beer.
"I do not know what will become of you,
Or of me and the money I have spent my life to earn.

"I will equip your voyage and buy you the ship,
So that you may explore the sea beyond your Foreland,
And find the passage to the Indies, there.
Incidentally,
(You will forgive the mention of it,
Since I know that such trifles do not trouble you)
If you find gold, you will bring me back a little
To pay for the fairy tale which will beggar me."

He got up, groaning, and from a curious cabinet carved
                    with strange knobbed heads,
Took down a Bible and a roll of parchments.

"On this Book, now,
(Which I suspect means little to you),
You will swear a bargain to bring me back a mermaid,
And perhaps a little gold.
And when you have sworn and roundly perjured your soul,
Then I will show you maps which I have gathered,
As I have pieced them up
From talking with other men who have come back from the
                    New World.
You know them, no doubt, but you have not talked with the
                    men.
You will make me another,
And I, no doubt, will thank my God and die
If you live to bring it back to me."

PART TWO

The body of William Tamfield, ship's boy from England,
Plucked from its chopped grave in the ice,

Stripped and cast aside by the curious savages,
Lay naked and pure in the naked purity of the snow.

"We are going on a voyage over an unknown ocean,
Into a strange land where there is gold enough for everyone,
And any man can pick up jewels sparkling on the ground,"
William Tamfield had said, to his little cousin,
Leaning on the gate before his father's house in Cornwall,
"I will bring you back a diamond as big as a cabbage,
And we will hide in the elm tree over the high road,
And drop it on the head of the first thief who rides by in
                    a great carved coach, serve him right, too!"

O far from Cornwall,
William Tamfield!
He lay for three nights, his hair turned softly golden by the
                    moonlight,
His body, icy and carved, fragile as a plover's, jeweled with frost,
Which the moon made spark upon him and upon the leagues of
                    lonely snow.
On the fourth night,
A lean white bear nuzzled him,
Found him frozen and passed on,
Having no appetite for that strange meat.

PART THREE

        How true a dream the dream of yellow metal is,
        Only that man can say
        Who is able to reach with his hands into the stuff
                    of the world,
        And weld to himself his food, his shelter, and the
                    unstable tenure of his flesh.

        O changeling son among the sons of man,
        Who sees in the coins that clink so richly in his

                    palm, no dream,
          But only an excuse for dreaming,
          An impossible cache
          Toward which to point his lonely footprints,
          Like the yearning of a cell to divide
                    upon itself!

I

Through the long summer of the second voyage, the ship crept
                    over the sluggish waters of the inland sea.
The terrors of the Mare Incognita passed in safety,
Storms ridden out, sea monsters unencountered,
She drifted northward, with flapping sails, along a monotonous
                    coast,
Until the muddy shore turned the current east again.
No passage there, no landing . . . Only
Flats, beginning to freeze, stretched westward, hummocked by
                    rocks,
Peopled by small seals and what seemed to be a curious kind of
                    melancholy bird
That cried heart-piercingly,
More than music, making the men long for home.

In October, when snow fell,
Thick flakes, wet, through still air, downward into slaty water,
A foot deep on the hatches, inches deep on the muffled rigging,
They sailed south again, with the first wind,
Anchored in a shallow bay whose shore was lined with willows
                    and stunted spruces.

This vast, closed gulf was all, then, that lay behind the
                    magnificent Foreland.
There is no gold, the captain thought, leaning on the
                    rail in the early morning
Watching the light grow over the impassible barrens.
I have proved that the Bay has no outlet to the Eastern Ocean,

But alas, poor Pieter, I have seen no mermaids
Now . . . He smiled a little grimly . . . Nor ever did.
At least, God give me credit, that was the only lie I told him.
I wonder if a man has ever looked upon a solitude more
desolate
Than this,
Yet one horizon farther, and I might find
What I have come so far for,
Pieter, his gold, and I . . .
He paused, not knowing a word for the desire in him that
                was not all for gold.

Boots thumped the planking behind him, and Minot, the mate,
Saluted him soberly,
Saying after a respectful interval,
"It is growing colder, sir."

"Yes," the captain said. "I have been standing here, mister,
Listening to the sound of cold."
He had not, yet he knew now that the *hushing* sound against the
                ship
Was not the tide of the Bay returning,
But the slushy beginning of the pale green ice
That makes in ocean water.

"It terrifies a man," said Minot softly . . .
He was plain-spoken, and he had sailed with this captain
                before.
"How quickly the cold will come in these latitudes.
Last year, when we were embayed for three weeks, you
                remember,
That, without the storm which by chance shattered the ice-floe,
We would have had much sorrow before we returned the ship
                safely home."

"Yes," said the captain. "But I think that a landing here will
                take no great time nor trouble.
From the look of this place, God has forgotten to make a

                    highway across it,
It is only late October, and those clouds will snow, I think,
                    before they freeze.
Tomorrow will see us safely headed for the Straits and ocean.
I will need the shallop and five men,
Raiburn, I think, had better come with me
Since he is beginning to be troublesome about returning home;
And provisions in the event that we should be delayed on
                    shore."
"The shallop is ready, sir," Minot said briefly.
But he was thinking, looking at the land before him,
That it was not a land, but only
What a man might harrow his mind with were he to try to
                    imagine his spirit's ultimate loneliness.
Where we cannot go, we cannot go, thought Minot.
I know bushes like that; they have branches
Only on the southern side, and that means great north wind
And cold to freeze the manhood off of us
Should we have the bad luck to be here to feel it.
Last year we had luck.
It might not be again.
By God, I'm hungry!
When I am back in Holland, God stiffen me if I don't buy
                    ten big yellow Dutch cheeses,
Hollow them out and put them end to end,
And sleep in them
By
God!

II

The barren had not frozen everywhere hard enough to bear
                    the weight of a man.
The captain and Raiburn, the second mate, with three sailors,
Two having been sent back with the shallop to the ship,
Instructed to wait for the party by day or a
                    fire on the shore by night . . .

Picked a precarious way from hummock to hummock,
Over salt ice which gave no warning of its weakness,
But in the soft places slithered away from underfoot
                    like slush.
By dusk they were soaked and cold, had gone only a short
                    distance inland, and
With the coming of darkness, soft flakes of snow began to fall.
In the night
Huddled
On the lee side of a snowy hummock,
The white flakes falling straight down,
They heard wolves howl, saw a few lean shadows moving silently
                    against the dark.

Morning seemed to come less from the clearing sky
Than from a pale upward shimmering of the snow.
The sailors stumbled forward,
Not reassured by the captain's promise that they would march
                    inland only until noon.
The slow daylight seemed not strong enough to dim the stars,
The pure air burned in their throats,
And they had voyaged for many months with promises.

At noon
They climbed the silvered slope of the low hill
That yesterday morning, from the ship, had been horizon,
And looking down
Saw nothing but the same snow-hummocked plain,
Leading away past the few wind-twisted bushes
To the same horizon of a far-off hill.

III

Minot, on the third day, ordered the anchor weighed,
Stood watching grimly while the great chain heaved,
At last tore free,
Raising with it a circular chunk of ice.

The ship heeled with the morning breeze
Sheared out of the ice which clung like a skirt around her,
Stood for open water
Away from the deadfall of the still, shallow cove
Which another day and night of freezing cold,
His judgment said, would spring.

He had done all a man could . . .
He had waited longer than he dared
Before he had sent Roberts, the third mate, inland with a
                    search party.
Now Roberts was back, shivering by the stove in the warm cabin.
They had crossed the first barren,
And had found no trace but some blood upon the snow,
The beasts of the barren had gnawed the bones white and clean.

Beyond that place
Nothing.
Only a narrow, obscured animal-track
Winding away endlessly among the hummocks,
They had followed it for a little,
But if human feet, before theirs, had ever made prints upon it
Something not human had obliterated them.
"It is quite useless to search for mortal men
Whom devils had snatched away into the high air."
Thus Roberts,
Coughing and shaking by the cabin fire.
"He would have followed any track," said Minot,
"That seemed to be a way across the barren.
And well you know it, damn you!
Wherever he is, he is not with any devil."

Even now,
Minot,
Standing on the deck, feeling the thickening icefield
Grind at the vessel's planks,
Feeling her slow and stagger,
Cursed Roberts bitterly,

Knowing in his heart that the man had done the best for
                    the safety of all,
Knowing in his heart
That the peril of all was now on his own body,
Who had waited too long after his hope was gone.

IV

The others gathered around him muttering,
And Raiburn at last mustered the words he needed
To ask the captain to turn back.

"Go back?" the captain said. "We shall go back
When I have found to what this pathway leads
And whether it was made by men or beasts.
I have not come this far to go back now with nothing."

"What treasure could we carry back with us?" Raiburn burst
                    out.
"Gold is a heavy stone,
And in any case,
There is none of that stone upon this snow.
You will have the lives out of us all if you do not return
                    to the ship today
And set the course for home."

"Go back to the ship if you will," the captain said.
"I am the master, but we are all men here now."
His eyes swept over the men, already not seeing them,
Already ranging the barren again for signs of an
                    unmarked track.

Raiburn glanced at his companions, then, fearfully, along
                    the way they had come
On which the early dusk was thickening.
"The man is a devil," he muttered,
"And the waste places of the earth are his natural home."

He took up his bundle and the three moved on after the
                    lean back stalking ahead of them in the gloom.

"And he would come back.
He is stronger than the three of us put together,
And when the food is gone, we'll die before he will.
Nothing can kill him but a musket-ball. Maybe that won't.
                    He's neither mad nor human.
By God," Raiburn went on, seeing the growing horror
                    in the eyes of the seamen,
"I think he is the devil himself!"

On the fifth day,
The track which was now no more than a covered dim
                    depression where a track had been,
Came to a definite end upon a mound
Where stood a small cairn, covered with snow,
Icicled,
Beyond it nothing but a white and pathless plain.

"No. Leave it alone, man!" said the captain sharply,
As Raiburn laid hands on the mound to tear it open.
"Why?" Raiburn spoke boldly, knowing the two seamen were
                    with him.
They were starving now, and the dread had been rooted
                    in them.
"A thing like this, so strongly built
Was surely made to hold some marvelous great treasure . . .
The winter stores of the savages, or their gold."
With a quick movement, he thrust his musket barrel among the
                    stones.
The captain started forward, but stopped as pried stones
                    fell at his feet,
Revealing the cairn's recess and three small images,
Carved,
Hideous beyond the dreams of man,
And made of stone,
Which must have been carried far, there being no rock

upon this tundra.
"You see," he said slowly, as much to himself as to
                            Raiburn,
"The treasures here are of use to the savages."

He stepped around the stones
To where he could look down on the plain of snow,
Stretching away as far as the eye could carry.
"We must go back now," Raiburn muttered.
"Now we must turn back."

"There was food there," he went on, hoarsely, to the seamen.
"I say he is the devil and he had turned the food in this
            cairn to stone.
Kill him!"

But the sailors stood dull, unmoving,
Staring down at the fallen cairn,
Their bodies like the bodies of sick animals
Who lie absorbed in languor, noticing nothing.

Raiburn stepped back,
Stumbling with a croak of horror into the snow.
He aimed and fired a single shot.
The captain fell.
Being a devil, he died simply and fought scarcely at all.

PART FOUR

On the pale cold evening when the ship fled through
            the Straits out of the Great Bay,
Minot brought a musket on deck, and fired a shot, cursing,
At the pinnacled cape which glittered above them, two
            thousand feet of rock and ice.
Raiburn came and stood beside him, and together their lean
            bellies yearned after the birds that thundered

up out of the crevices,
As the lean spirit of man might yearn after the plumage of
    hope vanishing out of its sky.
Food there to last the thousand league voyage home, and out
    of reach,
Things as frail as feathers had found the way to keep it
    out of reach.

Minot turned his back on the bleak capes, whose sharpness
Began to blur a little in the dusk and the ship's lengthening
    wake.
"If you and your two vermin," he said to Raiburn
"Had come crawling down the ice cakes a couple of days sooner,
We would have started home by now and out of this."
He spat overside into the spinning water.
"We did our best," said Raiburn smoothly,
"We could not have left the captain sooner to die alone,
And we had only snow to bury him in.
I say he was a devil. He could change food to wood.
He would have sailed the ship and us with it into a hell
    as hot as this was cold."
"Hold your tongue, man! Get below!" said Minot tersely.
"In God's name!"
But that night,
Eating the scanty, rotten rations,
The vision of a great yellow cheese kept swimming before his
    eyes,
And he was silent, thinking of Raiburn's words.

Under the remote stars the waters of the unknown sea
    shone with fire,
Dashed back in glittering flakes from the fur-splintered
    planks of the ship,
Drifting away astern like a pale highway leading backward
    to mystery and silence.

JOHNNY

Johnny was a good boy,
Not very good.
He did what was told him
As long as he could.

Where he went roving
God knows; but
He left me a kiss
For to keep my mouth shut.

Johnny sent his mother
A pink coral tree.
She put it in the parlor
For people to see.

A little dried sea horse
Was what he sent me.

PILLAR OF SALT

Over my window swing the planets
Their great, lone arcs across the sky.
The city, snarling in the mist
Exists, and God knows why.

Lot's wife, looking down on chaos,
Had no saving sense at all;
But in the midst of this am I
Striving to be methodical.

WHAT WE LEFT

In the fortieth millenium
After Christ's birth,
A research ship from Jupiter
Made it in to earth.
And forty archeologists
Digging with their picks
Found forty trillion tiny
Indestructible white sticks.

The boss archeologist
In authoritative tones
Said, "What a curious people!
These must be their bones."
Then forty more diggers
Wandering around
Found forty trillion juglike things
Lying on the ground.

Also indestructible,
White like the sticks,
Couldn't be mashed or bent
By hammers or by picks.

The boss archeologist
Spoke up again,
"These must be their stomach linings,
But of animals or men?"
So they loaded on the samples
So the home-folks could see 'em -
The PLASTIC PEOPLE'S fossils,
In the Jupiter Museum.

1

Mankind is like the fat cow
Stuffed with corn and clover,
That gives a good bucket of milk
And then kicks it over.

PROPHECY

Known for beauty
Near and far,
Much it matters
How fair you are.

Wise or foolish
Prudent or bold
Your children'll keep you
When you're old.

They'll soak the bread
For your aged teeth
And when you're dead
They'll buy you a wreath,

Plant your grave
With a flowered stem,
And when they're old
Theirs'll keep them.

DECEMBER - 15th

To whom shall I send some Christmas greens?
To the nation's children, short on beans,
With a bottle of ketchup to take the crunch
Out of the cost of a school kid's lunch?

To the U.S. Senators, all good will,
For the state of the budget on Capitol Hill,
Who, hearing the sound of the Christmas bell
Season's greetings, Joyeux Noel
Eyed the kitty for means and ways,
And voted themselves a splendid raise?

For any tax payer knows the lift
To a hard-working man of a Christmas gift.

So this I'll send: You've done it again.
God rest you merry, gentlemen.

OPINION

Christmas 1988

Ring welkin loud,
Put all aside,
Stick holly in
The casement wide.
Mortgage your pay.
Come all untied
For merry, merry
Christmas-tide.

What if the stores
Are full of junk
And "happy" New Year
Is the bunk?
Ring out, you bells,
Clunk, clunk,
Clunk, clunk.
Because the goose
Is in the pot
The buttered rum
Is nice and hot,
And auld acquaintance
Not forgot.

TO A CONTEMPORARY POET

Oh use the simple words
For God's sake, do.
I wade through swamps and jungles
Trying to read you.

Where do you begin
And where do you end?
A simple comma, somewhere
Could be your best friend.

Punctuation, after all,
(Or so it seems to me)
Is only a tool, easy to use,
And it comes free.

If sentences butt together
Like cats on a parlor mat,
I struggle to get your meaning
Whether it's this
Or that?

Have pity on your readers
For word gets around. It spreads
That all of us poets
Are a batch of eggheads.

THE HANG-DOWNS

There's a hill on Bartletts Island
So steep and high and round,
Where the Wendigo on his big flat feet
Makes tracks all over the ground.

Where the Dingballs ding at the Will-am-Alones
And the Sidehill Gougers ski,
And Dr. Pilgarlic with hair on his teeth
Lives in a hollow tree.

But the Hang-Downs, the Hang-Downs
Don't ever go near the Hang-Downs.
They're hard to see
And there's one to a tree,
And
They . . . hang . . . down.

On every end of a Dingball's tail
Is a great big bowling ball.
He'll ding at you once; he'll ding at you twice,
And brother that is all.
And Dr. Pilgarlic plays a game
On folks just passing through.
If he plays that game,
You won't be the same -
You'll have hair on your teeth, too.

But the Hang-Downs, the Hang-Downs,
Stay away from the Hang-Downs.
They're slimy and green
And they're seldom seen,
But
They . . . hang . . . down.

Big Tunk and Little Tunk live in the pond
As long as the moon is bright,
But let it be foggy and dark and still
They go tunk-tunk all night.
And the Aber-Nits creep out of the brush
To wiggle up your nose,
And Tobacco-juice-squirters lie in wait
To spit all over your clothes.

But the Hang-Downs, the Hang-Downs,
You better beware of the Hang-Downs.
You better run
Like a son-of-a-gun
Because
They . . . hang . . . down.

Now the Razor-Shins can kick at a tree
And whammo! down it whumps
If once they get a whack at your legs
You'll go home on bloody stumps.
And the Will-am-Alones go round all day
Sometimes the whole night through
Rolling poison toadstools into balls -
It's candy, just for you.
But
The Hang-Downs, the Hang-Downs
Don't fool around with the Hang-Downs
They're colder than ice, and they aren't nice
And
They . . . hang . . . down.

Oh, that hill on Bartletts Island
Is full of many things.
Some give great squeals, some roll on wheels
Some fly on big black wings.
On your lucky day, you might get away
From one of them, or two,
But you won't exist

And you won't be missed,
Or maybe you won't be you,
If
You run a-foul of the Hang-Downs,
The slithery, withery Hang-Downs
They won't move a hair,
And they'll be there,
And
They . . . hang . . . down.

OLD SAM

Where's old Sam
Saw the German submarine,
Rose up black
On a moonlight night?

Cussed thing came
Sneaking right by him,
Made a hissing, pooping sound,
Never showed a light.

Everyone, them days,
Kept lookout on the water,
World War Two
Only just begun.
Coast Guard said,
"Come and git us, running,"
Most took care, but
Sam took his gun.

Clouds in the sky,
Driving from the west'ard,
Moon dodgin in and out
Made it hard to tell.
Dark where the shadows were,
Bright in the moonpath.
Sam thought, later on,
He couldn't see
Too well.

There the thing was,
Swole out like a rooster.
Think the hens was watching him
The more puffed out he growed.
Kept on heading up the Bay
To'wards Fox's Narrows

To do what devilish actions
Only God knowed.

Sam got mad
When he thought about it,
And the more he thought about it
The madder he got.
"Them sons-of-hooers'll
Ruin Vinal Haven.
What they need
Is a charge-a buckshot."

Sam had a trawl-line
Half out of water.
No fish to speak of,
Wrong time of tide.
Didn't think no longer -
No time for thinking -
Grabbed up the trawl-tub
And hove it overside.

First time he fired,
Couldn't say he hit it.
Thing kept rambling
Not even fast.
Put down his shotgun,
Started up his engine,
Edged a little closer
And give another blast.

"Ha!" Sam hollered,
"How you like them apples?"
This time, bullseye,
Right in the red.
Thing went down
Like a busted iron hogsid,
"Sunk ya, by God!"
Sam said.

Daylight coming,
Flood tide making,
Clouds in the west'ard
Cooking up a squall.
Couldn't say he cared for
The look of that weather.
Better quit pooping round
And hunt for that trawl.

Then he saw the black thing
Back on top of water.
Not very far off,
And Sam turned tail.
Wasn't no submarine,
German or otherwise,
What he'd shot at
Was a damn great whale.

Sam took off
Like a gun-scairt sheldrake.
Throttle wide open,
Couldn't even pray.
His old power-boat
Walked on the water,
Just touched whitecaps
Most of the way.

Someone asked him,
"What was your hurry?
Where was the fire?
Who was dead?"
"Whale in the Bay
Getting kind of nosy.
Them things is dangerous,"
Sam said.

Where's old Sam?
He's still living,
Round eighty-seven,
Don't seem to fail.
He's a wild talker,
Tells a good story,
But he never says nothing
About that whale.

BILL CATES

Where's old Bill?
Got sick of trawling,
Smelling fishy,
Eating salt.
Didn't make a
Cent all summer.
Tried hard and
Wasn't his fault.

Last time out
Caught one old dogfish,
That was all, and
Bill saw red.
Didn't kill it,
Wouldn't bother.
Hove it overside
And said:

"You go back and
Tell your brothers,
Bill Cates is
Done and through.
This old free lunch
Counter's closing.
T'hell with it
And t'hell with you."

Bill Cates, he
Started inland,
Blistered his feet and
Lamed his knees.
Hiked up into
Fox Ears country.
Bought him a chain-saw
To cut down trees.

Country wild
And full of varmints,
Big old river
Ambling through.
And the boys in the camp
Filled him solid full
Of what ever that river
Could do.

"Fox Ears River
Now," they said,
"She's smooth as a
New tin can.

"Got what it takes
For ducks and drakes,
Ain't no place
For a man.

"Wild white water
Is what this river knows.
Looks back on what
She come from,
And on to where
She goes."

"Kind of still
Ain't she?" says Bill.
"Flatter'n a
Turkey platter.
I been around
Wild water some,
But I never see water
Flatter."

"Fox Ears River,
Now," they said,

"Got trout as long
As your arm.
You ever dream
That fish in a stream
Likely might come
To harm?

"You go fish
From a blowdown log,
Some dark September dawn,
And you'll find out
That all them trout
Has got outriggers on.

"Wild white water
Is what this river knows,
Remembers skulls
And sunken hulls
Of skiffs and gundalows."

"Well, dogfish,"
Bill said,
"As long's your leg,
Don't have any need
For such.
They got more to
Contend with,
And it don't
Bother'm much."

"Fox Ears River, boy,"
They said,
"She's silky-blue
And green.
Don't nobody know
What's down below
Only, it's cussid
Mean.

"Witches, says most,
Or someone's ghost
Creeping along the sand,
Or a poor dead girl
With her hair outa curl,
And an auger in her hand.

"Wild white water
Is what this river knows,
It ain't no freaks
That makes them leaks
And sets up
Undertows."

"Out on Old Man Ledge,"
Says Bill,
"Water's kind of white,
And a poor dead girl
With her hair outa curl,
Hollers out there
All night.

"Her name was
Sally Trumbull,
And she is good and dead."
But none of them
Seemed to listen,
Or hark to
What he said.

Bill stood it
Till December,
When the river
Froze up tight.
Far's you could see
Wasn't nothing,
Only flat and white.

Wild cats howled in the timber
Cold as a dead man's vest,
And nobody laid off
Bragging about
Which was the
Goddamned best.

Bill said,
"You take your river,
And shove her
Far's you kin.
I don't give a cuss
Where she's going,
And less of where
She's been.

"She may have ghosts
And creepies,
And witches,
Like you said,
But who could tell
The diff'rence?
The whole damn
Country's dead.

"Listen," he said,
"It's time you knew.
My name is Willard Cates.
And I'll bet five
Hundred dollars,
I can make it home
On skates."

The boys lined up,
The river bank.
They laid their
Money down.

"You stand to lose
Five thousand,"
They said, "You'd
Better drown."

And one said,
"Bill, don't try it,
That river'll
Kill you dead."
"Well, you can send
The money down
When I git back home,"
Bill said.

Fox Ears River
Comes from the
High country.
Above her lie
The dark old hills,
Below her lies
The sea.

And wild white water
Was what that river knew.
She opened up a
Breathing-hole,
Just as old Bill
Came through.

Out over the open water
He zoomed with a
Whistling whizz,
And the boys on the bank said,
"Jeez, he's walking on water!
Who does he think
He is?"

Where's Old Bill?
Got a lot of money,
New boat, new trawls,
All a man could wish.
He's out working,
Tough and mean
And stubborn.
Fishing Bartlett's Narrows
And cussing dogfish.

TEETER TUCK

Old Teeter Tuck, as reckless on the mast
As in a treetop, felt the wave-shocked plank
Leap under him, and, clutching rotten rope
Sprawled in an arc across the sky and sank.

Ice-cold and salt, the sea shut over him
Like a slammed door. His oilskins weighed him down.
He struggled upward, wondering grimly why
A man could come so many miles to drown,

And thoughts, not alien, troubled him. Should one
Meeting his death by water, think of wide
Purposeful waves, or souls? A rope sang. Then
Towering above, the schooner's crusted side.

The forecastle was merry in the gloom
Of lanterns winking through their ancient smut,
He clashed his glass, feeling around his waist
A red-hot circle where the rope had cut,

Visioning nothing, now his throat is wet
With good, green grog, his gurriest story told.
So many watches now, so many sleeps,
So many quintals stored below the hold.

"Give 'er a heave!" "Y'blasted mermaid, you!"
"Diving for fun, he was, to bring up bones!"
"What was y'after, Teeter?" "Hell, he dove
To swipe a kiss off old Ma Davy Jones!"

II

His line cut through the water furiously,
The while he braced his knees against the tug
A big fish gives for freedom. Bert spat out
Tobacco juice, advised him with a shrug.

"That there's a shark. You better cut your line."
"Swaller your bait. This ain't no old maid's tea!"
The line slacked suddenly; he saw beneath
A thick, swift shadow shooting through the sea;

And was aware, clamping his fingers tight
Around the gunnel of the foundered boat,
In water that holds almost nothing up -
Of Bert's small blue tobacco-tin afloat.

III

The cold cut through his jacket and his boots,
And found his bones. He saw the winter sky,
And through the wheel that froze his hands, the moon
Icy and yellow as a seagull's eye.

To one who had used that round and timeless moon
For sober kitchen clock as long as he
A world with scant beginnings and no end
To struggle for, should have no mystery;

Nevertheless, he could not tolerate
A dimness raised within him by the gold
And crystal reticence. He grumbled, and
For want of something better, cursed the cold.

IV

He gutted cod at sunset on the deck
With others, bloody-fisted, daubed with scales
Charley was tropic fire cooled in mist,
And Bill, a pleasant fat man, full of tales.

Bill had no silences. Perpetual
Small streams of perspiration coursed his fat.
The sins he had, little but magnified
He wore as lightly as he wore his hat.

Therefore, it seemed a punishment too great
Out of proportion, when he cracked a joke,
And the young tiger, Charley leaped and slit
His windpipe open with a single stroke.

And Teet who saw his own bespotted boots,
Casting an eye from crimson clot to clot,
Was somewhat muddled as his mind made out
A man's blood like a fish's, only hot.

V

The blue, familiar roadstead, lined with shore,
After the ocean seemed absurd in size.
He could not quite adjust himself to see
Water that stopped before his eyes.

And even on the dock he found himself
Braced from the shoulders down, as one who feels
The heave and sway of ocean under him,
And holds a vessel's deck between his heels.

Vessel or dock, it tilted crazily.
He could not get the rocking of a boat
Out of his head or what must be, again,
The clawing of the sea against his throat.

VI

Always, to ease his spirit's wayfaring
He had sailed windy water. Times between
There were few things on land he had not done,
Nor many places that he had not seen.

Now was a time to let his visions fade.
Thoughtful no more of ships or where they went,
He felt the fever vanish from his heart,
Came to his peace at last and was content.

VII

All afternoon until the fog came in,
On any last veiled gesture of the drowned,
The vessel sought some sign of Teeter Tuck,
Sunk in the ocean, out of sight and sound.

OLD GEORGE AND THE HALIBUT

Where's Old George
Caught the big halibut?
Damn thing weighed nigh
Two hundred pound.
Couldn't get him in the skiff
Wouldn't cut the handline.
All George could do
Was wrastle him around.

All day long
Hauling and holding
Sea made up and sun turned red.
Wind blew cold and dark kept coming.
Light went on on Bass Harbor Head.

"Well," said George,
"You ain't helpin any
And I ain't givin
A dad-darned inch."
Halibut heard him
Sunk down to bottom
Couldn't have budged him
With a cable and a winch.

Early morning
Come nice and quiet
Sun poked up
Like a diamond on a ring
Sky like gold and likely coulda been,
" 'n there" said George,
"That's a real pretty thing."

All night long
Line hadn't jiggled any
Laid there easy,

Never moved a hair.
George looked down,
Couldn't tell a thing
"Hey," he said, "Bud,
You still down there?"

George had had it
He was freezing
Yanked on his handline
Hauled in the slack.
Tied it to his rubber boot,
Set up his rowlocks,
Out oars and
Started rowing back.

Halibut shook up
Almost yanked his foot off,
Didn't want where he was going
And less of where he'd been
George never missed a stroke
Pulling and hauling,
Took eight hours
To tow the thing in.

Where's old George
Lived long after,
Lived to be ninety
And died in his bed
Anybody ask him
About that halibut,
"Like towing a mattress,"
Was what George said.

OLD HANNAH

Hannah, the storm being done, took down her shawl,
And softly, mindful of her husband's snore,
Stole with her basket down the moonlit path
To see in secret what had washed ashore.

Three days of wind had stripped the trellis bare
Of trumpet-vine. Autumn was cold and late.
A bird's nest on the path forlornly seemed
A summer frippery, all out of date.

She stamped her decent rubber on it. Then
Easing her body, with rheumatic twinge,
Came to the beach, nor saw, behind, the moon
Make ribald shadow of her, shawl and fringe.

"It's time to pile the punkins. The'll be frost
Before tomorrow mornin, I misdoubt.
If I'd ha' known how cold a night it is,
I'd ha' thought twice before a-venturin out."

The sea, far out withdrawn, the stricken beach
Left lonely to the moon, the whispered stir
Of sucker-shells moved something in her mind,
Bits of inspired gossip came to her;

Unthought of ways of getting ahead of folks,
A penny saved, the sucking pig grown fat.
"That pan I'll solder, and that tennis ball
Some youngone, now, will pay a dime for that."

Sure-footed as a cat, but not so light,
She plodded gravely on to where the beach
Ended in ledges and white pools of foam
The shrieking sea had left. Beyond her reach

She saw a gleaming; grunted; peered; and there
Stark in the moonlight, shining silverly,
Beauty forever kept from mortal eyes
Lay in a pool for Hannah's eyes to see.

She saw bright hair afloat on starlit shell,
A panicked hand that beat the hollowed ledge,
White, blood-stained breasts, a torn and delicate fin,
Scales, spattered out like jewels at the edge;

And, for a moment, while a thin voice cried
A piercing word she did not understand,
Her mind slipped sideways, seemed to lose itself
And tumble, with her basket, to the sand.

How had the old wives talked, who, dying late,
Had said a bitter name for what must be
In wait beyond unknown, unearthly foam
To keep their sailormen so long at sea?

Good, honest anger drove the frozen blood
Hot to her veins again. She caught a breath,
And crushed the terror clutching at her throat.
"You hussy! Scarin decent folks to death!"

She stooped and peered, remembering her God.
"You! With your finny tail and yaller hair,
And not a rag to hide you! How'd *I* be
Flat in a puddle with my bosom bare?"

There was one thing for decent folks to do
When devil's spawn like this should wash ashore.
"It ain't a human woman, it's a fish.
It's half a fish, and I've kilt fish before."

The claspknife from her pocket . . . then she chilled
For as she leaned above the white and gold

And shuddering thing, it watched her, in its eyes
Something as veiled as starlight, and as cold.

No, it was not a fish. She struck and fled
Clumping across the rocks and up the hill,
Leaving her knife to glisten by the pool,
Her basket for the rising tide to fill.

THE HARD LUCK OF OLD RANDALL

Old Randall was a fisherman
Who couldn't make a cent.
His gear would break, his warps would part
His fishhooks all get bent.

The crabs and whore's eggs et his bait
Before the lobsters could;
No matter where he set his traps
It never was any good.

    Go home, go home, old Randall,
    And set your traps no more.
    The amber leaves of autumn
    Are falling on the shore.
    Oh, soon will come the snow squalls
    The nights without a star,
    And if you fish in wintertime,
    You'll be worse off'n you are.

Old Randall, he kept going out,
And on one sunny day,
He found a blob of greasy stuff
A-floating round the Bay.

He said, "I've found some ambergris,
It sure smells awful strong."
But 'twas nothing but an old dead cow
That had drifted round too long.

    Go home, go home, Old Randall,
    This luck is not for you.
    There are no silver quarters here
    Nor pennies for your shoe.
    This is an old dead animal
    Come floating from afar.

If you don't heave it overboard
You'll be worse off'n you are.

He could not patch his rubber boots,
His wife she had no dress,
And all they et was mush and greens
To fill their emptiness.

But Randall kept on fishing,
Each day found him outside,
Till his poor wife could take no more.
She starved to death and died.

Stay home, stay home, Old Randall.
She's got no other kin
To wrap a towel round her head
And underneath her chin.
The neighbors they'll come looking,
They'll gather, near and far,
And if you leave her lying there
You'll be worse off'n you are.

That day he caught a halibut
Big as a parking space,
But when he hauled it up to look
It had his old wife's face.

And when he put a hand to her
The hook it up and bent.
The damn thing bit his finger off
And turned around and went.

Go home, go home, Old Randall,
Don't carry on this way.
The icy tides of winter
Are roaring up the bay.
The sea is loud and lonesome
It's heaving on the bar,

And if you keep on wearing out
You'll be worse off'n you are.

But Randall went another time,
And on that last, black day
A pirate ship sailed round the Point
And headed up the Bay.

His sails were red as dogfish blood,
His flag was mean and bold.
And Randall said, "This now's my chance -
He'll be gunnel-deep with gold."

    Go home, go home, Old Randall,
    And grundge yourself no more.
    The silver lights of evening
    Are lit along the shore.
    Soon will come the darkness
    The night without a star,
    If you run a-foul of Captain Kidd
    You'll be worse off'n you are.

But Randall piled the power on
His engine smoked and strained,
He chased all night till morning light
And saw that he had gained.

Old Captain Kidd came out on deck,
He wore a dreadful frown.
He cried, "Run out the cannon
And mow Old Randall down."

    Go home, go home, Old Randall,
    Go where you b'long to be.
    The gold is in the sunrise,
    It's shining on the sea.
    Old Captain Kidd's a marksman,
    He sights you from afar,

And if you catch his cannon ball
You'll be worse off'n you are.

Old Randall caught the cannon ball.
He felt the awful shock.
He bounced ten feet up in the air,
And sunk down like a rock.

Down in the kelp he saw the crabs
Creep out and wave their claws,
And his last words bubbled upwards -
"Well. I ain't no worse off'n I was."

THE TIRED APPLE TREE

Two neighbors fought a war, year in, year out,
Over who should have the apples from a tree
That marked their boundary line, or just about.
Neither knew, really, where that line should be,
But each believed with spirit, heart and soul
The tree was hers, and both were set like stone.
Whoever got there first, with pail and pole
Was getting apples legally her own.

As time went on, things went from bad to worse.
One lady got an eye as black as coal,
The other, mortally hurt, screamed out a curse,
"Murder! You tried to kill me with that pole!"
She dropped her own pole, grabbed her apple-pail,
And slammed her staggering neighbor on the head.
And the last blows that followed did not fail
To leave one dying and the other dead.

So there they lay. No one had given in,
Even when both were voiceless on the ground.
Whoever got her breath back first would win
Were their last thoughts, in this, the final round.

II

Then silence fell in the tree's shade,
As if the sun and the sky and the air
Had found the place where silence was made,
And under great wings had flown it from there.
No songbirds sang, no bees hummed the clover.
No sign of inquisitive circling crows.
Till a small brown cow came stepping over,
With a sprig of weed across her nose.
She said, "Hi, tree," and stood waiting there

Looking up at the laden boughs.
"I see you've got some apples to spare.
Seems they've left some, this year, for us cows."

Then a voice spoke out like an icy wind
Blowing over a frozen sea.
The leaves shuddered, loosened and thinned,
But not an apple fell from the tree.

"Each year I work a miracle, alone,
Send up my sap to break bleak winter's power,
Mother my boughs and call them all my own,
And on each new-born twig I place a flower.
I use the sun, the generous rain, the air,
Throughout the season my beautiful children grow.
Then my boughs are smashed and twisted, and there . . .
        there,
Chaos and bloody ruin lie below.

"My roots shrivel, my heart breaks,
At the evil curses, the blows and grapples,
What one of them snatches, the other takes.
You cannot comfort me with love,
And I am sick of apples."

"Don't feel like that," the brown cow said,
"It's not your apples that's to blame.
Now that them two old slumbags is dead,
Things'll never be the same.
Winter's coming with clean white snow
That'll bury this mess in a single day
Let your children go where they need to go,
You've still got your springtime debt to pay."

"I have no springtime debt," said the tree.
"I am leaving my life. I am wilting now.
There is nothing left. Nothing cherishes me."
"Me and my sisters do," said the cow.

"And one thing you don't appreciate,
Though when you're rested, you'll know it well.
Them two creeps killed each other's hate.
It's gone. It's frying with them in hell."

"Gone it may be," the old tree said.
"But hate lives in hell, it comes and goes,
It may spare an hour to bury its dead,
Then how many days of peace? Who knows?
How long stays the gift of the quiet nights,
When summer stars drift over the hill,
When the wheatfield glitters with firefly lights,
And the tick and the tock of Time is still,
Before the wind brings the rotten smell
Of old blood leaked from the centuries?
Hate is stirring again in hell,
The word comes in on every breeze.

"So my children shall stay on my shattered bier
While winter freezes and spring brings rot.
There shall be no leaves nor blossoms here.
Nothing shall grow on this cursèd spot.
My message I'll send through air and ground,
To carry my word to my kin, wherever
An apple tree in the world can be found,
Saying, 'Leave this place and be gone forever!
Nowhere on earth will your boughs be green,
Nor apple blossoms again be seen.' "

The brown cow gave a small choked cry.
She whispered, "Oh, no," then turned and fled
Back to the pasture field close by
Where her friends and sisters peacefully fed;
Where the pedigreed bull brought them all around
And led them close to the apple tree;
But to their pleading she made no sound.
A tower of icy cold was she.

III

That night in barnyards all over town
The stock went crazy, broke loose and ran.
They stopped the traffic, charged up and down,
Smashed what they could reach of the things of man.
The pedigreed bull roared his rage to the sky,
Like a tropical storm his thunder rolled.
His ladies performed disasters untold.
They demolished the fish market, passing by.

The townsfolk fled to what they could find;
Some even climbed the trees in the wood,
And the minister cried, "All hate is blind!
To where on earth has vanished our good?"

Then State troopers came and Police with guns,
The sound of gunfire filled the air,
And that was the last, as the story runs,
The battle for justice ended there.

IV

The pedigreed bull came limping over.
On the frozen tree trunk he leaned his head.
"The little brown cow will eat no more clover.
They shot her last night and she is dead.
They are killing the wounded cows today -
The useless ones whose milk has gone sour.
We willingly pay for the glorious hour
When we fought to show you our need of you
Because we love you, us cattle do."

He shivered and raised his battered head.
"They were always too much for us," he said.

The noble blast of his voice was hoarse,
The pride of his footsteps humble and slow,
The way of his going, the shambling course
Of a beaten beast.
The tree let him go.

V

All day the noise of the killings went
Up from the barns of the outraged town,
Over the sounds of quiet lament
That dwindled and ceased as the sun went down.

Silence spread on the falling night,
The chill of autumn blew in on the breeze.
The tree stood alone. Then a growing light
Came from the east, crept over the trees.
Shadows moved as the round, full moon
Shook off the earth and bloomed in the sky,
And the tree watched till she saw, too soon,
The silhouettes of her children lie,
The last apples ever to be.

"Abandoned to rot by a mother's hate,"
Said a cool voice that dropped from the sky.
"Hate is using you now to demonstrate
The power it has, just by passing by.

"I am the moon. I travel alone.
I sail here forever, now, as I must.
My face is winter, my heart is stone,
A dead planet of cold and dust.

"I have no feeling. I do not care
Where my light falls, on seas or shores.
What I was, is my own affair,
But you might guess that it could be yours.

"I am older and colder than you by far,
When I think of the sun, I find much good,
But your earth I see like a falling star,
Or a victim lost in a poisoned wood.

"My orbit is lonely, but this is my place,
Where I look down on you from above.
Over me is the safety of endless space
And I need no part of friendship or love.

"But your earth has plenty of both to give
For goodness and grace could be yours alone
If the evil cloud let your people live,
Not wrangle to death over some small bone.

"I am the moon. I have watched hate's grins
For centuries, seeing what it can do.
It never falters, it always wins.
It has come back. It is now in you.

"And I ask you, who will defend you now
With your outposts falling one by one?
You mourn the loss of a small brown cow
Whose love was needed and now is done."

In a wandering cloud the moon hid,
But showed as she travelled her ageless round,
The tree felt no change. Her apples did.
They twisted and shook and strained for the ground.
Those in the shadow were dim and cold,
But each in the moonlight glowed like a gem
Painted in stripes of silver and gold.
They seemed warm on the boughs. There was life in them.
And their voices called out in gusts of laughter.
"We may go late or we may go soon.
We may roost up here to some wild hereafter.
But who listens now to the foolish old moon?

Poking around in the sky up there,
From cloud to cloud, taking a peek,
Letting its notions out on the air,
To drop down on us, the lying old sneak.

"It's none of its business what we do.
We have no debt, and we may be few.
We are young, we are strong. Let anyone know
That we won't be told which way to go.
Apples shall be while the river runs,
While the rain falls cool on sweetened air.
We will blossom over the sound of guns.
If blood flows again, we will still be there.
So wait, sad tree, for comfort when
Your summer-time comes back again."